OUT AND ABOUT

A teacher's guide to safe practice out of school

SECOND EDITION

Maureen O'Connor

Illustrations by
Bryan Reading

School Curriculum Development Committee
ROUTLEDGE

First published in 1972 by
Methuen & Co. Ltd
2nd edition 1987
Reprinted 1988 by Routledge
11 New Fetter Lane, London EC4P 4EE

Transferred to Digital Printing 2004

© 1987 SCDC Publications

British Library Cataloguing in Publication Data

O'Connor, Maureen, *1940–*
    Out and about : a teachers' guide to
    safe practice out of school. —
    2nd ed.
    1. Visits by British school students.
    Organisation – For teaching
    I. Title   II. School Curriculum
    Development Committee
    371.3′8

    ISBN 0–415–02557–5

Contents

Foreword

This revised edition of *Out and About* seeks to encourage positive attitudes to educational experiences and opportunities outside the confines of the school buildings. Schools are increasingly recognizing the importance of providing learning experiences and opportunities out of school within the context of a broad curriculum. Positive attitudes to safety and to the clarification of curricular aims and objectives should feature prominently in the minds of readers of this book. Although the book is primarily intended for teachers, we believe there is much of value in it for advisers, parents, governing bodies, and all those involved in youth and community service.

We do not attempt to cover all eventualities, but wish rather to reinforce the notion that safety is more to do with positive attitudes than it is to do with volumes of words or regulations. The need for effective leadership, reaching collective decisions involving all parties, and a move towards more experiential learning strategies demand a high quality and calibre of staff.

Chapters 1 to 4 are essential reading in all contexts and chapters 5 to 9 are specific to particular activities although there is some overlap, which was thought to be advisable. Appendices are included to guide readers to specific sources of help and support and we would recommend they are used in connection with the relevant chapters of the book. Many agencies/organizations exist to provide the necessary information, help, and appropriate qualification in support of practitioners following curricular objectives which take their students out of school.

The advisory group has provided excellent support to the author. Our sincere thanks are offered to Maureen

O'Connor, the advisory group, Alan Siddall, Gordon Turner, and other SCDC staff who co-ordinated the various contributions.

We hope you have many safe and enjoyable educational experiences with more and more young people.

Keith McWilliams
Chief Executive, SCDC
June 1987

I

Learning out of school

There was a time when the school gates were clearly intended to keep pupils in and the outside world very firmly out. Even the design of our older school buildings reflected this philosophy: walls were high, windows deliberately above the line of sight to avoid distraction, the playground railed off from the street and the gates firmly closed from the first bell of the day to the last. The curriculum, it seemed, was rooted in an artificial world of textbooks and blackboards, and had little relationship with the community outside the school boundaries, let alone the countryside or urban environment beyond.

Times, thankfully, have changed – although some of the buildings have not. Even so, those lucky enough to enjoy modern school buildings now find themselves encouraged by the architects to look out through the plate-glass at the larger world outside. This undoubtedly reflects a new philosophy that views education and life as interconnected and inseparable. It is within this philosophy that teachers in school buildings old and new are working to build a closer relationship between schools, parents, the community, and the wider world beyond.

Much of the curriculum development work which has in many ways transformed both primary and secondary education over the last twenty years lends support to the view that the curriculum can be strengthened and enriched by involving pupils in activities outside school. Experience shows that enjoyment and motivation at all age and ability levels can be greatly increased by such curriculum development.

One consequence of this – and it is reflected in many educational developments through primary school to the whole philosophy of the new General Certificate of Secondary Education (GCSE) examination, with its emphasis on practical skills and communication – is that many more children spend far more of their time off the school premises. Visits may vary in distance and duration, from the infants' class outing to the local library to a secondary school's adventure holiday which may, these days, take young people as far as China or Africa. From all these excursions children and young people return with new observations, attitudes, ideas, experiences, skills, and enthusiasms.

An outside educational visit may deepen the pupils' awareness of the world they already know, so that a familiar environment may become an exciting and stimulating field for research, or it may extend their experience by introducing them to new environments, to fresh skills and to different social and vocational situations. Through such contact with the world outside the classroom, study within it acquires purpose and relevance and becomes more meaningful.

As Her Majesty's Inspectorate put it in *The Curriculum from 5 to 16* (Curriculum Matters 2, HMSO, 1985):

> In particular it is necessary to ensure that pupils are given sufficient first-hand experience, accompanied by discussion, upon which to base abstract ideas and generalizations. Teaching and learning might, for example, extend to using the local environment, undertaking community service and establishing contact with commerce and industry.

Recent years have also seen an accelerating growth and development of outdoor and residential experiences for the 14 to 18 age group, in particular through initiatives like GCSE, the Youth Training Scheme (YTS), the Technical and Vocational Education Initiative (TVEI), and the Lower Attaining Pupils' Programme (LAPP), as well as developments in assessment such as pupil profiles.

These are all exciting new developments, but they often take students into an unfamiliar environment and therefore carry with them implications for safety which need to be thoroughly thought through in the schools. Some activities may not have been envisaged when traditional guides and procedures for out-of-school activities were drawn up, and some may involve for the first time as leaders teaching staff who have had little previous experience of out-of-school work or a particular environment.

In particular, activities which rightly encourage experiential learning and much more initiative and decision-taking by learners themselves call for greater emphasis than ever before on the quality of leadership if they are to succeed educationally and be conducted safely.

Similarly, the Warnock Report and the subsequent 1981 Education Act on the education of children and young people with special needs within the mainstream of education have far-reaching implications for all those involved in organizing out-of-school activities. The inclusion of pupils with special needs in a much wider range of out-of-school activities calls for some re-assessment of how teachers prepare for and supervise learning off school premises. There is much sympathy for the notion of 'entitlement' for all children and young people to the whole range of educational activities: much less thought has up until now been given to how this entitlement may be enjoyably and safely provided.

Relatively new, too, is an awareness throughout society that we are all in some measure responsible for the care and preservation of our environment, in towns and cities just as much as in the countryside. This is also an attitude of mind which needs to be fostered as increasing numbers of children and young people are encouraged to move out of the school environment into the world beyond. In particular, pupils need to be aware that some areas of town and country are sensitive to over-use, that some habitats are rare and precious, and that much of our world needs to be conserved and may be damaged as much by over-use by those who care for it as by the more obviously destructive attitudes of developers, the thoughtlessly careless, or those whose behaviour is clearly anti-social.

In a publication largely written for teachers, readers will be aware that the value of out-of-school activities lies in their relevance to the pupil and to the curriculum: out-of-school activities form an integral part of the educational programme. Every visit should therefore be preceded by careful educational preparation. The pupils involved must know the aim of the visit, what it is intended to accomplish, and its place in the pattern of the school course. Equally important is follow-up work: the discussion, interpretation, collation and recording which enable pupils to understand the value and significance of the visit and which stimulate further development and learning.

Parents should always be consulted, and where there are pupils of ethnic minority origin there will need to be particular sensitivity in the planning arrangements. For example, some ethnic minority pupils may not be able to join activities after school or at the weekend because they attend community school classes; Muslim parents may be concerned about mixed social activities; other ethnic minority parents may be anxious about dietary arrangements. These matters are raised where appropriate in the book, as are specific considerations relating to pupils who have special educational needs. Out of school activities are valuable for all pupils and the social, gender and cultural mix of participants can itself be an important educational experience.

Safety, which is the major theme of this book, is far less a set of rules than a total attitude: no rule book can lay down guidelines for every unexpected event in every environment in which teachers and pupils may find themselves outside school. Indeed the purpose of many out-of-school activities, particularly those which involve young people in unaccompanied activities in the community, in preparation for the Duke of Edinburgh's Award for example, is to develop individual initiative and self-reliance. The aim of planning and preparing for every out-of-school activity must be to take the obvious precautions against the obvious hazards, and then to assist both the adults and the pupils involved to deal competently and confidently with the unexpected – whether it is the accidental separation of a child from its group on the London underground or the experience of an unexpected and potentially lethal blizzard on a shelterless mountainside.

Safety depends on the right attitude of mind, and the development of that attitude will be dealt with in more detail later in this book. But, as with all books offering practical advice, it is important to stress that schools and teachers have to adapt to the needs and capacities of the children in their own particular groups, and to the specific environment they face during a visit or expedition. And that, although the book is concerned with detailed planning and preparation, this should in no way overshadow the wider educational purposes of education out of school.

2

Some key questions for schools

This check-list may look intimidating, but it should be remembered that it deals with points which need to be considered over a period of time, and by other school staff as well as the designated leader of a visit. Many of the procedures will be initiated as a matter of course by the experienced group leader, in which case this section will provide a simple and convenient means of confirmation that the various stages of planning have been worked through. For less experienced leaders, or assistant leaders, the check-lists should provide a means of confirmation that nothing essential has been left out. In either case, no check-list should be regarded as definitive, and a careful written record should be kept of everything that has been proposed and agreed by all those involved. At the end of this chapter figure 1 (page 15), 'Thinking through the process', attempts to place these key questions within the context of an overall planning strategy.

Preliminary questions for the school, head, and governors

- Should safety education be a part of the whole school curriculum?
- What is the educational purpose of the proposed visit?

- Does it fit into the agreed curricular aims and objectives of the school?
- Is the amount of time to be spent on the visit justifiable in relation to its educational value?
- Is there a nearer or more convenient venue which would meet the proposed aims and objectives?
- Is sufficient time available to plan and prepare for the visit in class, and to organize suitable follow-up activities afterwards?
- Does the proposed visit fit in with departmental colleagues' plans for this class or group?
- What will be the pupil response to the proposal?
- Is the visit available/accessible to all pupils who would benefit?
- Have pupils had experience already which is relevant to the purposes of the proposed visit?

Questions for the group leader and colleagues

Personal issues

- Do I need any specialist expertise to lead the proposed visit?
- Do I have the experience and confidence to lead a group of this sort involving pupils, colleagues and other adults?
- Do I have the time needed for preparation and follow-up work?
- Do I have experience of this particular kind of visit?
- Do I feel competent to deal with the financial and insurance aspects of such a visit?
- Have I attended any INSET courses on the organization of school journeys?

Health and safety issues

- Do I have access to all relevant guidelines and advice on out-of-school activities from the local authority, governors and/or headteacher?
- Am I familiar with first aid and emergency procedures?
- Have I made the guidelines on health and first aid available to accompanying staff?
- Do I have access to any relevant health information on all pupils taking part? Have I checked record cards and spoken to the head of year/class teacher about possible health or medical problems?

- Do I have access to health information from parents?

Organizational issues

- Have I discussed the general proposal with the head, and, where appropriate, more experienced colleagues?
- Have I drawn up detailed plans for the activity and informed the headteacher, head of department and/or governors as required?
- Have I checked that suitable staff are willing and able to accompany the group?
- Have I considered the need to recruit other adult helpers such as parents?
- Have I prepared adequate information for pupils and their parents about the visit?
- Have I made adequate arrangements for contact in case of emergency?
- Have I arranged briefing meetings, as necessary, for pupils, staff, and parents?
- Have I costed the activity properly and made the necessary financial arrangements for collecting money, giving receipts, meeting bills, etc.?
- Has a preliminary visit been arranged where appropriate or possible? If one is not possible, is the visit wise?
- Has consideration been given to all potential hazards: activities, water, heights, fire, safety on the journey, etc.?

Questions relating to the head, governors, and LEA

- Has necessary preliminary permission for the visit been obtained?
- Has the necessary notice been given to the headteacher, governors and/or local authority?
- Have all necessary local authority guidelines been noted?
- Have the headteacher and/or governors had the detailed information required for formal approval?
- Have local authority or governors' guidelines on finance and insurance been met?
- Can the head make satisfactory arrangements to cover the

classes of teachers who will be on the visit?
- Have the head and governors offered the leaders of the visit adequate advice on matters such as finance and insurance?

Questions concerning colleagues

- Have staff who are suitable, qualified, and willing been found to take part in the visit?
- What particular expertise do they have?
- Can they be released from their usual school work and, if necessary, replaced?
- Are any other proposed adult helpers acceptable to other staff taking part?
- Have information and/or briefing been arranged for colleagues and other adult helpers?

Questions concerning pupils and parents

- Has a preliminary letter been sent explaining the proposed visit and soliciting support?
- Have the replies to the preliminary letters and discussions been assessed to ensure that the proposed visit is viable?
- Can a realistic number of families afford the proposed visit?
- Is financial help available for those who cannot? If not, should the visit go ahead?
- Is there a 'reserve' limit below which the visit cannot take place? If so, are families covered against loss of deposits by appropriate insurance?
- Has the proposed activity been discussed with pupils in class?
- Have pupils and parents been involved, where appropriate, in the planning?
- Have the needs of individual pupils (religion, diet, health, gender, behavioural and learning problems) been ascertained and allowed for in planning?
- Does the timing avoid the holy days or holy periods of different religious groups so that the visit is accessible to all pupils?
- Are there cultural constraints (e.g. about boys and girls mixing) which need to be considered?.

14

Figure 1 Thinking through the process

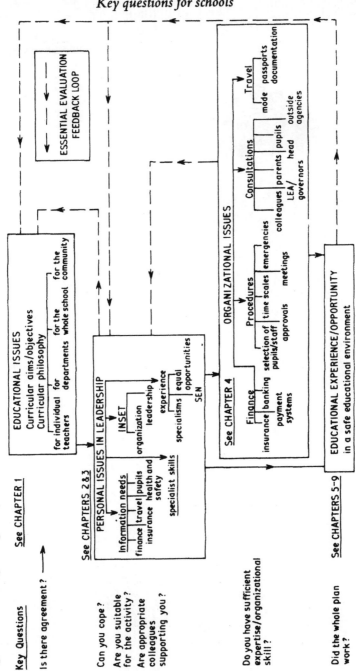

Key questions for schools

Key Questions

Is there agreement?

Can you cope?

Are you suitable
for the activity?

Are appropriate
colleagues
supporting you?

Do you have sufficient
expertise/organizational
skill?

Did the whole plan
work?

EDUCATIONAL ISSUES
See CHAPTER 1
Curricular aims/objectives
Curricular philosophy

for individual for for the for the
teachers departments whole school community

ESSENTIAL EVALUATION
FEEDBACK LOOP

PERSONAL ISSUES IN LEADERSHIP
See CHAPTERS 2 & 3

INSET
organization
leadership
experience
specialisms equal
opportunities
SEN

Information needs
finance | travel | pupils
insurance health and
safety
specialist skills

ORGANIZATIONAL ISSUES

Travel passports
mode documentation

Consultations parents pupils
colleagues outside
agencies
LEA/ head
governors

Procedures time scales emergencies
selection of meetings
pupils/staff
approvals

Finance insurance banking
payment
systems

See CHAPTER 4

EDUCATIONAL EXPERIENCE/OPPORTUNITY
in a safe educational environment
See CHAPTERS 5-9

15

3

Leadership

The educational success and the safety of any out-of-school activity depend crucially upon the leadership qualities and experience of the teachers leading the party. It is essential that, from the earliest planning stage, the role and responsibilities of the group leader be clearly defined and accepted by everyone taking part, and that, if the nature of the visit justifies it, a deputy leader be appointed with a clearly defined role and with the responsibility for taking charge of the party if the leader is absent, or in an emergency when the leader is unable to take charge. While a school party is away on a visit the legal responsibility for the safety of pupils lies squarely with the leader or with any other adult to whom specific responsibility has been delegated.

This means that the first step towards organizing any activity will be the establishment of a clearly defined chain of command which will hold in all circumstances and may well override the normal distinctions between staff, and between staff and other adults. The leader must have total responsibility and authority for the organization and supervision of the visit or activity: this will include the responsibility for planning and for liaison with the headteacher, and, through him or her, with the governors and the local authority, and with other staff and responsible adults accompanying the party, and with parents. It will also include the responsibility for the on-the-ground control and supervision of the group while out of school, even if the team includes the headteacher or other more senior members of staff. In an emergency, the safety of the party may well depend on this having been spelt out clearly in advance so that appropriate action is taken without confusion or hesitation in a moment of crisis.

It follows that teachers contemplating the organization of an out-of-school activity of any sort must first of all consider their own qualities and experience in a leadership role. In general, it is not wise for any teacher to take on the group leader role without having had some experience as an assistant on the sort of visit being considered. This applies to a half-day outing with a junior class to the local museum or park as much as a two-week residential adventure visit within the UK or abroad. Neither should be undertaken lightly, and the more complex and hazardous the proposed visit, clearly the more extensive the experience, and even training, a potential leader should have. Many local authorities now provide training courses for staff wishing to prepare themselves to take part in out-of-school activities in general, and there are specialist courses, leading to qualifications, for those wishing to supervise sporting and adventure activities.

Perhaps the first question a potential group leader has to ask when considering the possibility of organizing an out-of-school activity is whether they themselves have the necessary experience and personal qualities to do the job. And it is no reflection on their general ability as a teacher if careful thought leads them to decide that they are not experienced enough to carry the responsibility for this particular activity.

Crucial to the role of leader of any out-of-school activity is the ability to control and discipline children in a different environment which could be hazardous and which pupils may well find exciting or disturbing in some way. It is not unusual for children and young people on out-of-school activities to become nervous, travel-sick or frightened in circumstances beyond the teacher's immediate control. Their behaviour and readiness to respond to discipline may be very different from the way they normally behave in the

18

classroom or on the sports field with the same teacher. It may need a teacher of some confidence and personal resource to cope.

Prospective leaders need also to assess their own recent experience of out-of-school activities, any special skills they may need for the particular visit or activity proposed, and whether they have had, or can obtain, any training which might be required. Training and qualifications do not of themselves make a successful out-of-school leader, but there are activities, which will be discussed later in this book, for which they are essential.

One of the more difficult of the leadership tasks is undoubtedly to weld together an effective team of adults which may include more senior staff, parent or other non-teaching helpers, and possibly on some visits the partners of some of the participating staff as well. It may be important when building a team to discover the hidden talents of those taking part: their skills may not be immediately obvious. All must be regarded as full members of an integrated supervisory team in which roles are clearly defined and within which there is no room for accompanying 'holiday-makers', however recreational the aims of the visit. Headteachers will wish to verify on behalf of their governors and LEA that there are no 'passengers' accompanying a visit.

The relationships between the adults taking part in the visit may well be crucial to its success. Personal incompatibility can cause unwanted tensions, and so can a failure by the leader to clarify the duties and responsibilities of all the adults taking part. Ideally a group leader should have considerable influence on the selection of other adults, both teachers and non-teachers, so that some judgement can be made as to suitability and compatibility.

Pupils too should be involved, where appropriate, in discussions of leadership and the allocation of responsibilities during a visit. Senior pupils, in particular, have much to gain by developing their own organizational and leadership talents on an out-of-school visit, and should in any case be encouraged to develop self-confidence and self-reliance, one of the essential aims of such activities.

It will be the leader's responsibility to identify and define the purpose of the visit and its educational or other objectives, in cooperation with the other adults and pupils involved. Whatever is planned should be appropriate to the age, capability and needs of the children or young people concerned. All the practical arrangements should be sound, well-organized, and confirmed in advance. A preliminary visit is advisable to inspect the facilities being provided, particularly those for pupils with special needs, and to make contact with staff at the centre.

It will be the leader's responsibility to prepare both adults and children for the visit, and, in addition to the obvious paperwork, this will include the need for briefing meetings to allocate responsibilities to adults, in line with their qualities and experience, to answer practical queries, and to work out what may be quite vital codes of conduct for all participants. Before any visit involving an overnight stay it is also essential to arrange a briefing for parents and pupils, so that their queries and anxieties can be fully dealt with, and detailed arrangements clarified.

Equally it will be the leader's responsibility to make sure that any proposed visit meets guidelines for the organization of out-of-school activities laid down by the school's own governors or by the local education authority. At the same time, a leader should realize that guidelines can do no more than offer the minimum standards which the body concerned feels able to require. Clearly no school can offer less than the minimum standard of care or safety laid down by its authority. But it may well be that a group leader ought to conclude that the minimum standard is not good enough for the circumstances of a particular activity.

Suggested ratios of adults to pupils, and of men to women, for instance, which many local authorities now lay down in some detail, may not be adequate if a party includes a number of children with special needs, or if the proposed location or activities are particularly hazardous. There is an element of judgement involved in interpreting guidelines which depends crucially on the leader's own experience and knowledge of the children, the adult helpers involved, and the nature and scope of the visit. Leaders would be well advised to discuss ratios with their headteacher and governors before coming to any conclusions.

Similarly the allocation of responsibilities to other adults, and the working out of safety and emergency procedures for adults and children, will depend to a great extent on the leader's ability to assess the qualities and experience of everyone taking part. It may be reasonable to grant older children unsupervised time away from base, for instance, while younger or less able children might need – and parents may expect – constant supervision. It may be reasonable to allow some pupils the opportunity to work in groups without an adult, while other groups – possibly depending on their individual composition – would require a constant adult presence. Again the leader's judgement and detailed knowledge of the make-up of the group are crucial to the safety and success of the project. But if pupils are to be expected to work alone, or are to be given unsupervised free time during a visit, parents should undoubtedly be consulted in advance.

The organization of an out-of-school visit or activity may also involve the leader, possibly for the first time, in detailed financial responsibility for the group. Travel arrangements, accommodation, food, insurance, pocket-money: all may involve extensive paperwork, and the handling of large sums of money in advance of the trip or activity and while it is in progress. This is another area where previous experience and confidence in one's ability to cope with a major administrative task involving substantial sums of other people's money are of great advantage to the potential leader. The more complex the expedition, the more complex and time-consuming the accounting and booking procedures may be. School or local authority guidelines on accounting for out-of-school activities may exist, but again personal experience as an assistant group leader is probably the best preparation for any teacher thinking of taking on the group leader's role. In larger schools the leader may be able to call upon the experience and assistance of the school's bursar or administrative staff and seek to delegate some of the financial responsibility appropriately. The ultimate responsibility for the presentation of a satisfactory final statement of account for an out-of-school visit lies with the headteacher, who must satisfy the procedures required by the local authority's auditors.

Leaders also need to give some consideration to their own health and stamina before undertaking what may be the gruelling responsibility for a major educational visit. Planning should always include consideration of minimum standards of fitness and performance which will be required from participating pupils: water-based activities, for instance, may require a minimum swimming capability, and it may be necessary to give careful consideration to the physical and mental competence of special needs pupils before involving them in strenuous or demanding activities away from school.

There will always be unforeseen events on any visit. Some will be the sort of happy accident, the coincidence of people, place, and learning opportunity, which can make an educational outing most worthwhile. But there will also very occasionally be tragic accidents which could not have been foreseen. Some activities are by their very nature hazardous and an element of risk cannot be eliminated without detracting from the enjoyment and skill of the activity itself. Unavoidable accidents should be, and are, very rare. Most eventualities can be anticipated by the thoughtful and well-prepared group leader. When they cannot, tragic consequences can be avoided by leaders, supervisors, and pupils who have been well prepared to deal with the unexpected, as well as the expected, with confidence, competence, and calmness.

Most vital of all, perhaps, is the leader's ability to communicate the message which is intended to underlie the whole of this book: that safety out of school is not merely the effective drawing up and implementation of a set of procedures – however skilfully and thoroughly that is accomplished. It is much more the inculcation of an attitude of mind, a well-founded safety consciousness, which will ensure the maintenance of good practice at all times, however unforeseen the circumstances that may arise on a visit.

4

Planning a visit

It is a sad fact of professional life that the sort of spontaneous, spur-of-the-moment visit that most adults look back on with greatest pleasure is simply not an option for the class or group. As a professional, the teacher has a clear duty only to take children out of school with the full permission of parents, the headteacher, and possibly the local authority. The safety of pupils in a teacher's charge depends crucially on the meticulous planning of every stage of the visit.

Safety, in this context, does not consist merely of the absence of accidents but a positive state of mental and physical security which comes from the knowledge that all the teacher's responsibilities have been recognized and met.

Teachers in charge of a visit are responsible *to* the headteacher, the employing authority, and *to* the pupils' parents; and are responsible *for* the pupils in their care. Planning and implementation are two-way processes which involve the school and local authority on the one hand and the pupil and family on the other.

Legal responsibilities

It is well known that teachers stand 'in loco parentis', to use the legal term, for children in their care. This means, in

25

effect, that teachers are required to act reasonably, as a careful parent would, even though they have charge of far more children than any family would regard as reasonable. Teachers' responsibilities are clear enough. They must take all reasonable steps to ensure that every child under their control is protected from unacceptable risks. The law does not expect the impossible. No person can protect a child or children from every conceivable hazard. The expectation is of 'reasonable care', but, if that can be proved in law to have been absent, a claim for compensation can arise. Although the careless or negligent act may be that of a teacher, in all probability the legal proceedings will be taken against the employing authority on the basis of the employer's vicarious liability for the negligent acts of the employee committed during the course of employment. A check should be made to ensure that the employing authority would also accept a similar responsibility for the negligent acts of accompanying adults, where the authority has agreed that they should be members of the party. This would not necessarily preclude legal proceedings being taken against individuals.

Nor is this duty of care limited to the teacher in charge of a party. When acting as assistants, the usual duty of care will fall on all accompanying adults on a visit. The accompanying adults will share in the duty to take all possible steps to prevent foreseeable accidents to their charges. In some circumstances, other teachers or accompanying adults may quite properly be left in charge of pupils during a school visit, but in this case – or in circumstances where the leader may delegate responsibility to the staff of an adventure or residential centre – it is still the leader's duty to make sure that those who take charge of pupils are properly equipped and briefed to do so. The overall responsibility will still rest with the group leader, the responsibility for a particular child with the adult actually in charge of that child.

It is because of legal liability, and in the light of tragic accidents on school visits, that an increasing number of local authorities now issue quite detailed guidelines and instructions for teachers undertaking out-of-school activities. It is up to the potential group leader to inquire what the employing authority's requirements are before the planning for any visit starts. Local authority regulations may well require, for example, that the consent of the school's governors or of the chief education officer be sought for specific kinds of out-of-school activity.

The responsibility for ensuring that any proposed visit complies with local authority or school regulations lies with the headteacher. The head may well delegate the general oversight of a visit to another member of staff, but he or she remains legally responsible for seeing that the group leader is adequately experienced and, if necessary, trained. The headteacher needs to ensure that preparation for the visit has been thorough, that supervision levels conform to local authority regulations and are in all respects adequate for the nature of the visit, and that the school has been made aware of all the detailed practical arrangements which might be needed in an emergency.

It is the group leader's responsibility to ensure that all adult members of the group are clear as to their legal responsibility for the safety and well-being of the children in their charge. There should be no scope for misunderstanding on this score on the grounds that some adults are 'only there for the holiday', or that some are parent-helpers and not teachers. Nor should there be any doubt in any adult's mind as to who is responsible for particular aspects of safety procedures (checking children back from group activities, for instance), or as to the precise chain of command which is in force during all out-of-school activities. Children's safety will depend on the fact that all adult members of the party have been fully and clearly briefed before the visit begins.

Financial aspects

Funding

It has usually been assumed that it is perfectly legal for a school to charge pupils for most out-of-school activities, whether they have a high recreational element, or whether they are directly relevant to a course of study. In terms of charges, no distinction has been made between the Austrian ski visit and the geography field visit to Wales.

However, a recent ruling by the Local Government Ombudsman, yet to be tested in the courts, suggested that a charge made by a local authority for the attendance of a sixth-form A level student on a residential field visit was illegal because it contravened Section 61 of the 1944 Education Act which forbids the charging of fees for education in maintained schools.

The crux of the Ombudsman's ruling is whether or not the field visit was an essential part of the student's education. That is a question which may arise ever more acutely with the introduction of the General Certificate of Secondary Education courses, which assume a much higher practical content than previous examination courses did.

It is now clear that teachers will have to look very carefully at the costing of out-of-school activities in general and course requirements in examinations in particular in the light of possible new government legislation.

Handling money

It is in the handling of money that many teachers may feel most insecure when leading a visit for the first time. Careful planning will be necessary to enable the actual visit or visits to go off without worry 'on the ground'. More experienced colleagues and the headteacher or, in larger schools, the bursar or administrator should be available to offer advice on the proper procedures to be used for a long and costly visit.

The first thing for teachers to remember when handling money on behalf of parents or the school is that while it is in their possession they are responsible for its safekeeping and may have to make good any accidental loss. By taking charge of money, teachers are responsible for handing it over in full to whoever it was intended for: travel agency, coach company or airline. And it is as well to be aware that the responsibility is a personal one: if a loss occurs, the local authority may be very unwilling to make a claim on its insurance on behalf of the teacher responsible.

The second point to remember is that all money collected on behalf of the school must be able to be satisfactorily accounted for at all times. In order to avoid what may be a distressing and embarrassing dispute over the accounts, it is necessary to record all transactions with absolute accuracy at the time they take place, and to keep that record carefully. The more expensive the activity being organized, the more vital careful accounting procedures become, but even the handling of quite small sums of money can cause embarrassment, and may cause the teacher to be out-of-pocket at the end of the day. It may seem tedious to issue receipts for the 50p per pupil required to take a class on a bus to the local museum, but it is worth the extra effort to avoid muddle and acrimony when a child claims to have paid, and no record can be found, or when a total sum falls short of what it should, and the teacher has to make up the difference personally. Similarly, when sums of money are handed over to colleagues or to the school office, a receipt should be requested.

For a major school visit, it may be necessary for the group leader either to use a school bank account or, if this is not possible, to open a special school account requiring two signatures on cheques to hold and dispense the visit's funds over a period of time. The important point is that money collected for school purposes should never be muddled or confused with the teacher's own personal funds, either in a bank account or in cash. It is vital not only to be honest, but to be seen on paper to be honest as well. Local authorities require headteachers to confirm that accounts for school visits and journeys have been properly audited.

The use of a bank account provides an easily verifiable record of sums paid in and paid out but, where a large amount of money from different sources is deposited, then it is advisable to keep a careful record of exactly where the component parts of the total come from: for instance, it is wise to keep a record of which pupils' payments go to make up a total sum deposited. Bank statements offer another way of verifying the written records the leader keeps personally, and allow for an early warning of any discrepancies – a bouncing cheque, for example, or some other error in a payment.

Finally, it is wise to keep all the records intact for at least a full twelve months after the end of the financial year in case of a query.

Costing a visit

Keeping the accounts is only part of the successful financial planning of a visit or activity. The first consideration is the necessity to travel and, if there is a need, how far is it necessary to travel and by what means, and where and at what cost the party will be accommodated away from school if the visit is a residential one. The more complex the activity, the earlier the start which has to be made on costings, which may mean obtaining quotations from competing firms of travel agents or travel companies. Accurate costings should include incidental expenses like bus or underground fares between stations, baggage-handling charges, airport taxes and an allowance for emergencies such as a breakdown, if travelling by road, and delay at an airport or port if travelling overseas. It is also usual to make some allowance for administrative expenses, and for possible changes in the exchange rate for foreign currency if the party is travelling abroad, and, wherever possible, the cost of a pre-visit to a residential site. The fear of overcharging parents should not deter teachers from making sure that the charge for the visit is completely adequate: a refund can always be made to parents if a 'profit' is left at the end of the day, and that is far preferable to teachers finding a deficit to be met from their own pockets when the final account is drawn up.

The collection of cash

Parents should be informed at an early stage when money is due. For a major visit it is quite normal to expect a substantial deposit on booking, and then instalments for the rest of the cost. They should be told at what point it is no longer possible to withdraw from the booking without incurring a financial penalty, and this will probably depend on the travel agent's own cancellation rules. Receipts must be issued for all cash received.

Insurance

One of the recommendations of the inquiry into the Land's End tragedy in 1985 was that local authorities should now advise their headteachers and staff on their insurance practice for out-of-school activities. Practice varies from one local authority to another, so it is vital to check with the headteacher on local guidelines, and the extent and adequacy of local authority insurance cover.

No school visit should take place without adequate cover. Precisely what is required will vary according to the nature of the activity. But, whatever the cover provided, the group leader should be familiar with all the terms and exclusions in the policy document. The following cover should be considered, bearing in mind that 1 and 2 are possibly covered by the local authority, and that 3 to 8 almost certainly will not be:

1. *Personal injury.* Many local authorities cover their own employees and approved volunteers for personal injury, but they do not extend this insurance to pupils. This should be carefully checked with the local authority, and parents should be informed precisely what is and is not provided. Parents should be advised of the desirability of taking out their own personal injury insurance for their children not just for school visits but also to cover children in the event of accidents during team games or even in the playground.
2. *Public liability.* This is insurance against the risk of an award of damages against the group leader or any other supervisor, leader, assistant leader, or official accompanying adult for death, injury, or illness suffered by another person, not necessarily a member of the group.
3. *Medical and related expenses.* This would cover the additional costs incurred by the group as a result of the illness or injury of a group member: for instance, extra travel or board and lodging costs if a group member had to remain in hospital after the main party had returned home, or the cost of

transporting an injured person home. Medical insurance is a necessity for any group travelling abroad where arrangements for medical care involve the payment of doctor's or hospital fees which may or may not be recoverable later.

4. *Extra expenses.* Insurance can be obtained to cover any unforeseen extra costs on a visit, caused, for instance, by strikes or transport cancellations.
5. *Personal baggage.* Insurance can be obtained to cover loss or damage to personal property, and for loss of money.
6. *Hired equipment.* It may be necessary to make special arrangements for the insurance of hired equipment or clothing.
7. *High-risk activities.* Standard insurance policies normally exclude high-risk activities like climbing, hang-gliding, etc. Separate insurance is essential if such activities are included.
8. *Cancellation insurance.* For an expensive visit, it is wise to include cancellation insurance in the package so as to avoid heavy financial loss to the school or to individual families if either participation by an individual or the whole visit has to be cancelled.

Organizations such as the National Confederation of Parent Teacher Associations offer comprehensive insurance cover to parents.

Travel arrangements

The choice of the mode of travel – mini-bus, coach, train, boat, or plane – will depend to a large extent on the distance to be covered and the cost. Some packages organized by school travel agencies will not allow any choice. In other cases, particularly those involving relatively short journeys, the leader will have a relatively free hand to decide how to get a party from A to B and back again.

General questions

1. Are there enough qualified adults accompanying the party to supervise the group while travelling, allowing for the fact that some methods of travel pose more problems than

others, or are more difficult to supervise? For example, there are far more ways for pupils to get into mischief on a Channel ferry than aboard an aeroplane; it is particularly easy to become lost or confused on the London Underground; a double-decker bus will require a supervising adult on each deck.

2. If a mini-bus visit is being considered, are there sufficient drivers with a valid mini-bus licence available for the journey concerned? Are all the drivers fully conversant with the regulations on mini-bus use, especially if the bus is to be taken abroad? Have they been reminded to carry their licence and insurance details with them?

3. Has the school already drawn up, or have the group leader and colleagues considered, a suitable code of pupil behaviour for the method of transport chosen? Do pupils themselves understand why they need to observe certain rules on standing or moving about in a moving coach so as to avoid being thrown if the vehicle brakes sharply?

4. Has the leader considered the need for toilet and refreshment stops in relation to the route and the duration of the journey?

5. Have parents been asked to provide their children with travel-sickness tablets if necessary, including enough for the return journey and for excursions during a residential visit?

6. Have plans been drawn up to discuss the particular method of travel with pupils, particularly if the journey is a long one, and if the mode of travel is new or unfamiliar to some of the group? Will anyone be travelling by Underground, by Channel ferry, or by air for the first time?

7. Have all departure and arrival times been double checked? Have arrangements been made for possible delays, and have parents been notified of all these facts?

A visit on foot

Many local out-of-school visits can be made on foot, but leaders should not underestimate the dangers of taking a group of pupils out into busy streets, however short the actual journey. The following check-list is helpful:

1. Have pupils been reminded of the road safety rules in the Highway Code and Green Cross Code?
2. Pupils should be instructed to walk in pairs, with a supervising adult, or, if this complies with local authority regulations, with senior or responsible pupils at the head and rear of the line.
3. Pupils should be kept under adult supervision at all times, and it is particularly important that, if a section of the group stops for any reason, the whole group should stop so that no pupils are split off from the main party.
4. Full use should be made of crossings and subways for crossing the road, but if none are available a crossing place should be selected that offers good vision in both directions, and pupils should be clearly instructed as to whether they are to cross in pairs or simultaneously on the teacher's instruction, and to wait in an orderly way at the other side of the road until the full party has crossed.
5. Children should be instructed how to seek help if they become lost or separated from the group at any time.

Travel by bus

1. Travel by public service bus may be suitable for a school visit outside rush hours if the service is regular and convenient.
2. Discipline is the responsibility of the teacher in charge, not the bus conductor, and on a double-decker bus, it may be necessary to have two supervising adults on the visit.
3. It is usually convenient for the teacher to collect fares before departure, pay for the whole group, and retain the tickets for safe-keeping.
4. Pupils should remain in their seats during the journey and not approach the exit of the bus until it has stopped.

Travel by mini-bus

1. There are strict regulations governing the use and driving of mini-buses, with which the local authority and school should be familiar. A group leader should check these regulations before deciding to make use of a school, or other, mini-bus.
2. A mini-bus driver is personally responsible for checking the

fitness and condition of the mini-bus before departure.
The following practices are illegal:

a) obstructing the driver, or any entrance, exit, or gangway;
b) using the mini-bus with broken or dirty windows;
c) filling the petrol tank with the engine running;
d) carrying inflammable or dangerous substances in
   containers.

A driver's inspection before departure should include:

- fuel, oil, and water
- tyre pressures, tyre condition, and wheel nuts
- brakes and brake lights
- lights, horn, and indicators
- windscreen wipers and washers
- reflectors
- vehicle body and internal fittings

EEC regulations on mini-bus drivers' hours are stricter than
those in the UK and are enforced by regulations requiring a
tachograph, which monitors driving, to be fitted to the
vehicle. The Assistant Masters' and Mistresses' Association
publish a leaflet, 'The school minibus and the law', and the
Royal Society for the Prevention of Accidents (RoSPA) a
booklet, *An Introduction to Basic Minibus Driving*. These cover
practical points and legal responsibilities and are highly
recommended for anyone leading or driving a mini-bus
group.

Travel by Underground

Many school pupils, even those living in London, are
unfamiliar with the Underground system, which from the
point of view of a school party is undoubtedly the quickest
method of travel around the capital. Pupils should therefore
be carefully prepared for a visit by Underground and
instructed on how to cope if they become separated from
their group.

1. Tickets can be purchased in advance from London
   Transport and this avoids queues at ticket offices or

automatic machines. The group leader should retain and surrender the tickets for the whole party, unless it is necessary to pass individually through automatic barriers on entrance to or exit from the system.

2. Groups should move together with a supervising adult at the head and rear of the line.
3. All members of the group should be aware of the procedure to follow if an individual or part of the group becomes separated from the rest, e.g. if a lift can only accommodate half the group, or if members fail to board a train and are left behind at a station. As individual pupils are unlikely to be carrying their own tickets it is important that a rendezvous system should keep the whole party within the Underground system until they can be re-united.
4. Pupils may be confused or unnerved by the steepness of escalators, or by the crowds: they should be marshalled carefully at the top and bottom of escalators and on station platforms.

Travel by car

The carriage of pupils in a teacher's car can cause insurance problems, even if no direct payment is received. Teachers should check that their car insurance policies specifically include a clause which allows them to use their cars for business purposes. Teachers are legally entitled to use their cars to carry passengers so long as the vehicle cannot carry more than eight people, any money paid for the journey covers only the running costs, and any arrangements for payment are made before the journey commences.

Parents or other adults who volunteer to carry pupils as passengers have the normal responsibility of all drivers for the safety of their vehicle and those in it. A group leader, however, should make sure that volunteers and their vehicles are suitable, that acceptable numbers of pupils are allocated to each vehicle, and that pupils are instructed to behave responsibly while passengers in a volunteer's car. They should particularly be instructed as to the dangers of distracting a driver while the car is in motion. As part of the visit arrangements parents should be asked to give their written consent for their child to be carried in a private car with, if at all possible, the driver named. The leader and headteacher must ensure that the driver is properly insured for carrying passengers.

Travel by rail

The normal procedure for a school party is to reserve a compartment or coach for a train journey. This enables the group to stay together, and simplifies supervision throughout the journey. The station supervisor can normally inform the group leader where the reserved coach will stop, so that the group can assemble in the right place on the platform before the train draws in. Train travel carries its own inherent dangers, and a strict code of conduct should be agreed before departure and discussed in detail with pupils, some of whom may be unfamiliar with train travel. This should include rules for behaviour on the platform, for boarding, and leaving the train, during the journey and stowing luggage. To avoid annoyance to other passengers, it may be necessary to include rules on movement within the train to the toilets and buffet, and on the use of radios or cassette recorders on the journey. In older trains, it may still be possible to open windows and doors while the trains is in motion, and the danger of this should be drawn to pupils' attention. On arrival, pupils should be asked to stay in their seats until the train has stopped, and an adult should supervise the opening of train doors.

Travel by coach

Coach transport is relatively cheap and convenient for many school outings, and many schools have a close relationship with a coach company with which they deal regularly. However, familiarity should not be allowed to breed contempt, and care should be taken to check booking arrangements and instruct pupils carefully on a code of conduct on all occasions. This will need to include a ban on moving around the coach while it is in motion and on the opening of windows and doors, and should include arrangements for litter and for dealing with travel sickness.

The group leader should check the position of the emergency exit and first aid kit on entering the coach. Toilet and refreshment stops should be carefully supervised, and children checked carefully back on to the coach. It is wise for teachers to sit in different parts of the coach to facilitate supervision during the journey.

The following safety check-list is useful for coach and bus travel.

- Never attempt to get on or off a moving vehicle.
- Use handrails especially when carrying luggage.
- Stow luggage carefully on racks: heavy articles should go in the boot or on the floor, on the driver's advice.
- Do not put head or arms out of windows.
- Do not throw anything from windows.
- Never run about in a moving bus or coach: a sudden swerve or stop could cause a fall.
- Do not talk to the driver except in an emergency.
- Do not pass on steps or stairs.
- Fasten belts or coats that could get caught in doors when getting off.
- Never attempt to get off a vehicle except at an authorized stop.
- Never attempt to cross the road from near a stationary vehicle.

Travel by sea

The level of supervision needed aboard a ferry will depend upon the age of the party members: older pupils will wish for some freedom of movement to use the varied facilities of a modern boat, but should be particularly warned not to buy alcoholic drinks either in the bars or in the duty free shops. Customs allowances should be drawn to the attention of older pupils: the importation of drink and cigarettes is restricted to adults.

Clear instructions should be given to all members of the party about the stowing of luggage, and assembly at a fixed point at a fixed time before disembarkation.

Travel by air

Many children and young people are now quite familiar with air travel, but group leaders should remember that a plane journey may be a new experience for some, and that some members of the party may be nervous about flying. The following points are useful at the planning stage:

1. Children paying less than full fare have the same baggage allowance as adults.
2. Special meals can often be ordered in advance for children on a long flight.
3. Long flights can become boring and plenty of in-flight reading material, puzzles, and games are useful.
4. Pupils should be given a clear explanation of the airline's rules on hand baggage and how it should be stowed on boarding.
5. Members of the group should be asked in advance if they suffer from any medical condition which could affect them during a flight.
6. There are restrictions on what can be carried on aeroplanes and these include bans on inflammable materials such as toy caps, fireworks, etc. The airline's instructions should be followed carefully.
7. Customs regulations should be explained in advance.
8. A code of conduct should be drawn up to cover pupils' behaviour while aboard the aircraft so as to minimize annoyance to other passengers.

Activity planning

The activities proposed as part of a visit often require a substantial amount of planning in order for the visit to go ahead smoothly. The following check-list may be useful.

1. Have sufficient details been obtained about the availability of the activities proposed (e.g. opening and closing times for museums, parks, etc.) and the need for advance booking.
2. Is the activity centre used to dealing with school parties? If not, close liaison with those in charge is advisable.
3. Has a party from the school made a similar visit before? If so can previous staff expertise be tapped?

4. Is special equipment or clothing required?
5. Is advice or supervision available on the spot?
6. If National Parks are being visited, has advice been sought from the National Park Schools and Youth Liaison Officer?
7. Is there useful or essential literature for staff and students on the activity proposed?
8. Is a preliminary visit by the leader and/or other staff advisable to check local hazards, e.g. water, cliffs, flat roofs, etc., which may not be inherent to the activity itself?
9. Is any serious preparation or training required for the proposed activity? If so, can it be provided locally in the time available? For instance: a visit to the local dry ski slope; a short walk in hiking gear for those not used to walking boots; classroom discussion on suitable clothing for a visit; the viewing of videos on the areas to be visited; practical work setting up tents, using primus stoves, etc.
10. Have contingency plans been made?

Health and safety requirements

First aid

At least one adult accompanying a school party should have some up-to-date knowledge and experience of first aid and on longer visits should be responsible for making sure that an adequate first-aid kit and manual are accessible at all times. Other adults should be instructed to follow the advice of the first-aid expert in the event of an accident or emergency until professional help is available. In many situations a knowledge of what not to do is as important as a knowledge of what to do. Detailed advice on first aid is available from specialist bodies such as the British Red Cross Society and the St John and St Andrew's Ambulance Association.

Medical precautions

Pupils proposing to take part in any school visit, particularly involving an overnight stay, should be required to provide details of any medical conditions which could cause problems during the journey or while away from home e.g. a susceptibility to travel sickness, allergies or asthma, regular requirements for medication, etc. Some local authorities provide standard forms to obtain such information and also consent to emergency medical treatment if needed while on a visit.

Girls should be reminded to make adequate arrangements for sanitary protection during the visit. Emergency supplies should be carried with the first-aid kit.

The school should provide parents with early notice of any vaccination or injection requirements for visits abroad.

Group leaders should familiarize themselves with the arrangements for medical care in any overseas countries to be visited, and with any particular hazards which might arise in countries further afield. Advice can be obtained from the DHSS on both these matters.

AIDS

There is considerable concern about the AIDS virus. It should be understood that people with the AIDS antibody do not constitute a health hazard to other people in normal circumstances. However, in case a party should include a carrier, all supervising adults need to be aware of the situations in which there is some risk. These are described in the advisory documents produced by the Department of Education and Science (DES) and the National Union of Teachers (NUT). The documents include advice on general hygiene precautions and accident procedures where a carrier of the AIDS antibody is present.

Fire safety

On visits involving long-distance travel and overnight stays, the group leader should consider a code of conduct for fire safety and ensure that all members of the party know what action to take in the event of fire and know how to raise the alarm if they discover a fire.

All adults should be aware of the dangers that can lead to an outbreak of fire: e.g. unguarded fires, cigarettes, matches, lighters, inflammable liquids, paraffin heaters, boiling fat, stoves or camp fires too close to tents, and faulty electrical appliances or wiring.

Pupils should be particularly carefully supervised if there is any obvious risk of fire, such as when cooking, when using a stove or heater, or when around a camp fire. Codes of conduct should ban items such as cigarettes and matches.

On arrival for an overnight stay or on a preliminary visit, if one has been possible, group leaders should familiarize themselves with fire-escape arrangements and if possible arrange a fire drill for the whole group. All fire safety rules should be strictly observed throughout a visit.

Emergency procedures

Accidents, illness, and unexpected delays can cause emergencies on even the shortest school outing, and procedures should be worked out in advance and notified to parents to cover all eventualities. The need for urgent communication between the party away from school, the school, and some pupil's homes may be a two-way one, so contact points, with contact addresses and telephone numbers, should be listed clearly and notified to all who may need them.

Many local authorities lay down specific emergency procedures for school parties as part of their general regulations for out-of-school activities. If not, the following points may be helpful to a group leader planning a visit:

1. In a serious emergency involving injury or death, the group leader's first responsibility is to the victim, and then for the safety of the rest of the party. If the leader is occupied in dealing with a victim another adult should be delegated to look after the safety of the rest of the party.
2. Police and other appropriate authorities should be informed as soon as possible.
3. Everyone else who needs to be informed about the emergency should be told as quickly as possible through official rather than unofficial channels. In some circum-stances the police will undertake this duty and contact next-of-kin.

4. Once the immediate emergency has been dealt with and all other members of the party are safe, the leader should ensure that the headteacher and local authority are informed of what has happened.
5. The group's insurers will need to be notified quickly.
6. It is sensible for the leader and any witnesses of an accident to write down as soon as possible all the relevant details while they are still fresh in the memory. A note should be made of names and addresses of any witnesses or other contacts who may be helpful later.
7. An accident report form should be completed as soon as possible.
8. Legal liability should not be discussed or admitted.
9. Statements should not be made to the Press without prior advice from the headteacher or local authority.
10. Emergency procedures should be drawn up in advance and all adult members of the party made familiar with them before departure. Special procedures will be needed for visits involving adventurous activities and those in wild or inaccessible country (see Chapter 9).

Home–school relationship

Most parents these days appreciate the value of the increasing number of out-of-school activities schools organize. But, when children are taken, or sent, to school, the parents of primary and junior secondary age groups naturally assume that they will remain on the school premises for the whole of that school session or day unless parents are informed otherwise. It is therefore always wise for a teacher to notify parents of the intention to take children outside school, even if the visit is only a short walk down the road to the local park or library. More seriously, accidents can and do happen in even the most apparently innocent environments, and at the very least an unpleasant dispute could arise if a child were hurt when off school premises with a teacher's permission but without a parent's knowledge. It is even more vital to inform parents, especially of young children, if a visit is likely to interfere with the normal home-going arrangements after school.

Precise details of departure and arrival times should be given so that special arrangements can be made by parents to collect children or be at home when they arrive. For any visit formal written permission should be sought from parents to take children off the school premises. For regular local visits, some schools merely inform parents of their current practice at the beginning of the school term or year, but it is always advisable to obtain such general consent in writing. For major excursions it is likely that the local authority will provide standard consent forms, which must be completed by parents.

But there is a great deal more to home–school liaison than the simple seeking of formal permission for a visit. In educational terms, it is important that schools explain to parents how out-of-school activities play a part in the scheme of work or examination syllabuses, or why work experience or community work projects are felt to be of benefit to the pupils concerned.

Early communication about any proposed visit or scheme of work out of school is essential. This may initially be a letter to assess the amount of interest that a particular visit might generate if it were arranged. Once a firm course of action has been decided upon, a letter of invitation for pupils to take part should go home, carrying details of the precise nature of the activity, the proposed timing, and, if applicable, the cost to parents. Even at this stage it is sensible to remind parents that in some circumstances financial help may be available to families who cannot afford the cost of the visit. This is particularly important if the visit is an essential part of the syllabus, in which case the local authority may be under an obligation to fund the activity.

The more complex the visit or activity, the more information will need to be provided for parents, and the more detail a group leader may feel is needed on individual pupils: on any medical problems, for instance, or any emotional difficulties a child or young person may have on a visit away from home, possibly for the first time. For residential and overseas visits it is highly desirable to organize one or more meetings for participating pupils and

44

their parents so that final arrangements can be clarified and queries answered before departure.

The passing on of essential information between home and school in both directions should be in writing. After the inquiry into the tragedy at Land's End in 1985, it was recommended in the Garrett Report that parents should be informed of:

1. The name and address of the destination and any other centres to be visited.
2. Time and place of departure and return and arrangements for collecting and dispersing children.
3. Full travel arrangements, including estimated time of arrival on return, and what arrangements will be made if delay occurs.
4. Details of the proposed activities and the arrangements for supervision generally and specifically during designated activities.
5. The composition of the party and details of the name and contact address(es) of the group leader.
6. Details of other accompanying adults.
7. Financial arrangements.
8. Arrangements in the event of cancellation.
9. Details of pocket-money advised.
10. Staff responsible for handling money.
11. Full details of insurance cover.
12. Any inoculations which may be necessary or advisable.
13. A check-list of clothing and other equipment needed.

In return, depending on the nature of the visit, the school might ask for details of how to contact parents or other family members in an emergency, details of the child's health and fitness and any medication being taken regularly, and any religious beliefs which might affect diet or medical treatment. On the latter point, the leader should ask for specific guidance from parents, and inform them in writing of what action will be taken in an emergency. If this is not acceptable to the family, the leader should seriously consider whether the pupil concerned should be included in the party. On a visit involving an overnight stay it is wise to ask parents to sign a consent form for emergency medical treatment for children under the age of 16, especially for visits abroad where hospitals may refuse to operate without such consent.

Many local authorities have their own standard forms for these purposes.

5

Non-residential
visits

Short out-of-school visits are organized for pupils of all ages and abilities. Well integrated into the curriculum, they provide an exciting and stimulating experience for whole classes or smaller groups of children. Increasingly out-of-school activities are being demanded as part of the work expected for candidates for the new General Certificate of Secondary Education.

But whether a 'visit' merely involves taking a class just outside the school gates to conduct a traffic census, or away from school for a whole day by public or private transport, group leaders should be fully aware of their responsibilities for the safety of the group at all times. Careful planning and close supervision is always essential. The headteacher should be consulted, and for more ambitious visits formal approval may have to be sought from the governors or LEA, even for the briefest out-of-school activity. The head carries overall responsibility for the safety of pupils during the school day and should always be consulted about any departure from the premises within school hours. And it is the head who is responsible for arranging 'cover' that might be necessary for a teacher absent from school with pupils for a period of time.

Even a short visit may also require a certain amount of logistical rearrangement for the rest of the school. Children who are not going on the visit may need work set in advance.

The school meals service may need to be informed of the absence of an unusual number of children on the day of a visit, and the caretaker informed of what is planned. School bus arrangements may need to be checked to ensure that children who rely on buses to return home will be able to do so conveniently after the visit. Even on the shortest trip, arrangements should be made for a contact point at school during the day (or, if necessary, somewhere after school hours) in case of accident or delay.

Consultation with parents

Parents generally expect their children to be on the school premises and under supervision unless they have been specifically informed otherwise. It is always wise to obtain parental consent to take pupils out of school, even if only for an hour or so, although some schools and local authorities obtain general consent for modest out-of-school activities from all parents at the beginning of the school year or when children start school. The headteacher should be consulted about whether consent for any particular activity is necessary. If parental consent is sought, the information circulated to parents should include full details of the visit proposed:

1. The type of visit and activities planned.
2. The date and times of departure and return. (This is particularly important if a group is expected to arrive back at school after the normal time of closure or at some dispersal point other than the school.) Primary age children should normally return to school after a visit so that they can be collected by parents; secondary children may be allowed to return home directly if parents have been given prior notice of this arrangement, and have agreed.
3. The mode of travel and an emergency contact number in case of unexpected delay.
4. The arrangements for supervision, and the names of teachers and other adults accompanying the trip.
5. The cost and arrangements for payment.
6. Any special clothing or footwear, or refreshments required.

A form of consent should be enclosed to be signed by parents and returned to the school. Local authorities have their own forms. If necessary advice may be obtained from your professional association.

Classroom preparation

Classroom preparation is essential even for the briefest out-of-school activity. Every pupil should know the aim and purpose of the visit, what activities are planned, and how they are to be carried out. Time should be allowed for the study of background material, the preparation of worksheets and questionnaires, and instruction on the use of route plans, or Ordnance Survey maps, if appropriate. The journey itself can form a useful part of the educational experience. Purposeful and productive classwork following the visit will only arise out of structured and thorough observation while the class is out of school.

Pupils should also be carefully prepared for the safety aspects of the visit. They should be warned of all known hazards – and reminded that some hazards cannot be foreseen. They should be instructed to stay in a group at all times, unless given specific instructions otherwise, and even older pupils should not be allowed to leave the group singly but always in twos or threes. They should also be instructed about behaviour in particular situations likely to arise, such as crossing a busy road, response to a recall signal such as a whistle, or action to be taken in an unforeseen emergency.

Clothing and equipment needed for the trip must be clearly stipulated: it is as unsatisfactory to have a child overburdened with an unnecessarily heavy bag as to find one undertaking a survey or census without paper and pencil. Care should be taken in the issuing of, say, clipboards to make sure that pupils have them when they need them, and do not mislay equipment on the journey. For indoor and some outdoor visits the wearing of school uniform is useful for purposes of identification. Comfortable low-heeled shoes should be worn for any trip which involves much walking. Robust waterproof shoes or boots and waterproof outer clothing are required for country visits. Rules may have to be made on the carrying of cans and bottles as part of a packed lunch, and pupils should be reminded not to leave litter.

In general, rules for behaviour out of school should follow on naturally from what is expected on the school premises: groups should move about in a quiet and orderly way and behave with consideration to adults and other children they may meet on the trip. A reminder should be given about the need for particularly respectful behaviour in some locations e.g. religious buildings or graveyards, and silence in others, e.g. libraries. A clear code of conduct should be laid down before every visit and pupils' responsibility for their own behaviour emphasized.

The following points on specific locations may be helpful.

Historic buildings and sites

Large numbers of ancient monuments, from prehistoric hill forts to stately homes of the seventeenth and eighteenth century, are regularly open to the public all over Great Britain. Opening times and admission charges vary and should be checked well in advance. School parties often qualify for concessionary rates. Guidebooks, leaflets, and slides are often available and can be obtained in advance to help with classroom preparation.

Churches, cathedrals, temples, synagogues, or mosques should normally be visited by school parties only by prior arrangement, taking into account the times of services. Whether parties are taken round by a guide or a teacher, pupils should be reminded that the general public expects appropriate behaviour in a place of worship. Permission should always be obtained for brass rubbing.

Some large sites and buildings offer conducted tours but the success of a tour for a school party depends crucially on the ability of the guide to communicate easily with children in the age group concerned. If possible, a teacher should always check on the suitability of a guided tour for the particular group concerned before committing a group to a guide.

Archaeological digs

Most children are fascinated by archaeology and eager to join in what they may regard as a 'treasure hunt'. They need to be warned against disturbing or picking up fragments on an archaeological site, and against obstructing the diggers in their work.

Digging and the collection of objects on a site must be undertaken only with official permission from the local museum or archaeological association as well as from the landlord or tenant of the site concerned.

Museums

Many museums now have an education department which will assist schools wishing to visit the museum (or use the facilities in any other way, e.g. by borrowing objects) and will provide explanatory literature and talks or lectures on some topics relevant to the exhibits. The education department should be able to assist with the preparation of worksheets and advise on the most suitable parts of the museum to visit. Some museums provide rooms where school parties can undertake detailed work, and many now have refreshment facilities which would be useful on a half-day or full-day visit for older pupils. Younger pupils often find museum visits tiring and may not benefit from more than an hour's visit at any one time.

Close supervision of pupils on a museum visit is essential. The more traditional museums may have highly polished floors; glass display cases and exhibits alike are often fragile. Even where pupils are on a guided tour or are attending a lecture given by museum staff, the responsibility for discipline still rests with the teacher. Modernized museums may provide active displays, audio-visual demonstrations, etc., which will also require careful supervision of pupils and co-operation with museum staff.

Seashore visits

Local knowledge is essential for safety at the seaside, and local experts should be consulted about tides, eddies and currents, cliffs, estuaries, quicksands, and the safety of beaches and rivers for swimming.

Urban studies

An increasing number of school subjects at primary and secondary level involve pupils in active study, completing surveys and questionnaires outside the school premises. Teachers contemplating such activities should make themselves familiar with the area where pupils will be working, and especially with any hazards such as dangerous junctions, derelict buildings, unfenced water or railway lines, etc. about which pupils should be specifically warned. Supervision is particularly difficult if pupils are to be free to move around, and the area within which they are free to move must be clearly designated. In this case pupils should be warned about specific dangers such as traffic, or the risk of attack or interference in lavatories, subways, etc., and instructed to stay in groups, preferably of three, at all times. Educationally, too, group work is often preferable to individual assignments in a strange environment, especially with younger pupils. Clear instructions should be given on the time and place where pupils must reassemble, whether they have completed their assignment or not. Unless they are working very close to school premises and are of secondary age, pupils should not be dismissed before the normal school closing time.

Pupils working in urban areas should not inconvenience other pedestrians or drivers of vehicles in the vicinity. With senior pupils it may be convenient to release them to work out of school in small groups without continuous close supervision. Younger pupils will need supervision as a group. Pupils working unsupervised should be provided with adequate plans or maps of the area, and instructed what to do in the case of an emergency.

Country and farm visits

A clear code of behaviour (see the Countryside Code) should be laid down for groups visiting rural areas. Children and young people from towns may be unfamiliar with many of the less obvious hazards involved, and these should be explained.

In a relatively wild rural area, such as a country park or on open hill or moorland country the danger of a sudden deterioration in the weather should be anticipated, and a clear recall procedure laid down. If the party splits into smaller groups the leader should ensure that each has a watch and that the time and place for reassembly are clearly understood. The danger of exposure and exhaustion should be explained in case of a sudden deterioration of the weather in exposed conditions.

Procedures for walking along country lanes and footpaths should be established in advance and the group should be kept together, without stragglers, at all times.

Private land may only be crossed with the permission of the owner, unless it is crossed by a public footpath. In any case, the party should be strictly controlled so that no damage occurs to crops, fences, or stream or pond margins, no animals are disturbed, and no litter is left. If specimens are being collected – only with permission in nature reserves or National Trust property – teachers should ensure that only the minimum required is taken. Sketching or taking a photograph is often preferable. The danger of poisoning from unfamiliar berries, fungi, and sprayed crops should be explained to pupils.

Groups visiting farms should be kept small so as not to interrupt the farm work unnecessarily. Particular hazards such as tractors, machinery, haystacks, cesspits, and silos should be pointed out, and pupils should be instructed how to approach farm animals in an appropriate way. It should be remembered that children from urban backgrounds may never have seen farm animals at close quarters before.

Unexpected hazards can arise when a group has stopped for relaxation or refreshment. Approaches to icecream vendors or refreshment kiosks should be carefully supervised if there is also access for vehicles.

Swimming should never be allowed without parental permission, in the sea, rivers, or (particularly) canals. If swimming is allowed, look-outs should be posted to watch the swimmers and a person with a life-saving qualification should be present. Pupils should never be allowed to wander near cliffs, caves, rivers, or other water. Even with supervision, these are the places where tragedies can occur.

Charity walks

It is dangerous to walk on main roads, especially in heavy traffic, or on roads without footpaths. All roads are dangerous in the dark. Schools should consider very carefully whether to become involved in activities for charity which are as inherently dangerous as some charity walks appear to be. If it is agreed to participate in a sponsored walk, the police should be informed in advance of the proposed route and their advice sought on safety. If sponsored activities are being considered, playing field runs or sponsored swims serve the same purpose and are very much less hazardous than walking long distances on public roads.

6

Residential visits

The educational value of offering all children and young people the opportunity of residential experience is now widely recognized. Living and working together offers opportunities for social development for children of all abilities, including those with special needs, which are not normally available in day schools. There are, in addition, all sorts of practical reasons why a particular course or aspect of the curriculum may require pupils to spend some time away from home and school: from field studies trips for GCSE and A level examinations to intensive sports, 'adventure activity', and music or creative writing weeks or weekends. Leaders always need to be clear in their own minds about the main curricular purpose of the visit, but should at the same time be aware of the unique opportunities inherent in any residential visit for learning experiences which cannot be provided in school, such as camping and cooking, and simply coping away from parents and friends and the normal, often urban, environment.

The social benefits of a residential visit may be less easy to measure than the academic or physical gains derived from intensive work in an environment without distractions. But, for most young people, the social benefits of a visit away from home should never be underestimated. While living and working together pupils develop a high degree of social awareness so that by the end of many residential courses many know themselves, their fellow pupils, and their teachers or leaders more thoroughly – and with greater understanding – than before. Personal relationships may have been tested under new (possible more demanding and difficult) conditions, and individual young people may have become more aware of their own abilities and limitations, and their responsibilities to and for other members of the community in which they find themselves. Many individual teachers and leaders comment on the beneficial effects of a residential visit for pupils from the most difficult and disadvantaged backgrounds.

Many local education authorities have established their own residential centres both for field studies and for adventurous activities. School parties also frequently make use of facilities provided by commercial centres for young people, by the Youth Hostels Association, and by commercial campsites, hotels, and other forms of accommodation. The first task of a group leader is to assess the suitability of the accommodation and other facilities provided at the centre or site for the proposed visit. In coming to a decision it is helpful if the leader can contact another school/club or other organization which may have previously used the centre being considered. Leaders should remember that Her Majesty's Inspectors have no right of access to centres and facilities run by commercial organizations so that their quality is not necessarily assessed in any way by educationists. However, some centres do invite local authority advisers in, and individual local authorities should be able to advise schools on which centres have been seen by their staff and which have not, and whether previous parties from the LEA have already used the facilities. Leaders should always enquire whether the premises have a fire certificate and request details of fire escapes and arrangements for the evacuation of the premises in an emergency.

Preliminary visits

A preliminary visit is regarded as essential by many local

authorities and experienced group leaders. If such a visit is impossible to arrange, the leader should consider very carefully the advisability of the visit, and consult with other leaders who have taken parties to the centre concerned. In any case, it is vital to obtain full details of:

- the type of accommodation available and suitability for children with special needs if appropriate;
- the exact location and the nature of the surrounding area;
- whether or not there are resident staff and what roles they fulfil (domestic? instructor? etc.);
- what activities and equipment are available;
- the cost for pupils and accompanying adults;
- the details of the domestic arrangements, e.g. the size of bedrooms/dormitories, the accommodation for staff (of both sexes if the group is a mixed one), whether bedding is provided, the catering arrangements or, if camping is proposed, the availability of cooking, washing, and shopping facilities on site or nearby.

Only with all this information can a leader and assisting staff make an informed decision about the feasibility of the visit.

If particular activities are to be organized for the group by the centre staff, the leader will also need to have full details of the activities proposed, the qualifications of the resident instructors, and special clothing and equipment required by participants.

The British Activity Holiday Association (BAHA) is a relatively new organization, which now includes most large operators. It has adopted a code of practice covering safety standards and incorporating a bond of guarantee to cover the unexpected closure of a centre. Centres should always be able to provide full details of their own safety rules and codes of conduct for residents. Specific local authority approval should be obtained before pupils are taken to any centre run through BAHA or any other independent organization.

Most local authorities now lay down detailed guidelines on the organization and conduct of school visits in general and residential visits in particular. It is the responsibility of the leader to obtain such guidelines and draw up plans in line with them, in close consultation with the headteacher and governors. It may well be that the local authority will lay down specific staffing ratios and levels of qualification and experience for teachers taking part. The LEA may insist on special insurance cover for particular out-of-door activities, and require to be informed of, and to approve, the nature and extent of such visits before plans are finalized. Financial assistance for pupils whose families cannot afford the cost of a visit may also be available through the local authority.

Once a booking has been confirmed, close liaison between the school and the centre to be visited is essential. If other schools or organizations will be using the centre at the same time, it is advisable to contact their group leaders to discuss matters of common interest and concern. It may be sensible, for instance, to make sure that visiting parties of similar age are expected to conform to similar codes of conduct on matters such as bedtime.

Home–school liaison

Home–school liaison is of particular importance when organizing a residential visit, especially if any or all of the group are going to be away from home for the first time, or if any or all of them have special educational or social needs. Parents will naturally be anxious that the visit is well organized and adequately supervised, and children and young people themselves may have anxieties about staying away overnight which will need discussing with staff and parents, possibly together at a preparatory meeting.

Information for parents of pupils taking part in a residential visit should include details of:

- the educational aims and objectives of the visit;
- the type of course and the activites planned (including details of any adventurous activities proposed);
- the date and duration of the course, including times of departure and return;
- the names of the leader, accompanying staff, and other adults;

- methods of travel, including the name of the travel company, if any;
- supervisory arrangements at the school and at the centre;
- whether the visit is a necessary or merely a desirable part of the normal curriculum;
- the approximate cost of residence and transport, and the expected method of payment (i.e. date for payment of deposit, full fee, etc.) and precisely what the cost covers and does not cover;
- a suggested minimum amount of pocket-money;
- details of insurance to be effected, and precisely what is covered and not covered by the policy (parents may wish to take out their own personal injury insurance for the child);
- details of clothing and personal requirements and any special clothing or equipment required for activities, plus a list of prohibited items;
- code of conduct: details of the behaviour to be expected from pupils participating, including rules on smoking and alcohol;
- the full postal address and telephone number of the centre;
- advice on the desirability of regular correspondence and/or telephone calls, especially for children away from home for the first time (though the use of the telephone needs careful thought);
- any proposed visiting days, with times and travel directions.

- A consent form for the visit and a medical information questionnaire should be enclosed for parents to complete.

Staffing

The selection of teachers for a residential course demands careful consideration. The number of staff needed will be related to the specific course and activities proposed, to the age, ability, and sex of the pupils (at least one teacher of each sex should accompany mixed groups) and to the staffing, if any, at the centre, paying close attention to local authority guidelines on supervisory ratios. The teachers selected should be those who have relationships of trust, respect, and understanding with the pupils concerned and who appreciate and accept that their responsibilities will extend far beyond teaching or activity periods into leisure-time and night-time supervision. They should have the experience and ability to make a positive contribution to the course and to foster, through personal example, a sense of responsibility and reliability in all their pupils. Specific qualifications may be required in, for example, first aid, mountain leadership, or life-saving.

If other adults are to accompany the party then their selection is equally important, and similar attributes and qualities should be sought. In no circumstances should adults be allowed to accompany a school party for a holiday. An ill-assorted group of adults accompanying a party can soon exert a negative influence, and it is sensible if teachers and other adults know each other reasonably well before undertaking a residential visit together. It is also important to ensure that all adults accompanying the party meet the pupils before departure. Both teachers and non-teachers should be particularly carefully briefed on their duties and responsibilities before departure, particularly when night-time supervision and supervision of leisure activities round the clock will be required. Clear chains of command for all times and all eventualities should be laid down in advance.

The selected teachers, and particularly those undertaking residential work for the first time, should be carefully briefed. All staff members should understand the educational and social aims of the course and know what is expected of them. They must be informed of their legal liabilities and of the protection afforded by insurance arrangements. They should know what residential accommodation is provided for the pupils and adults, what medical facilities are available at the centre, what equipment is available for indoor and outdoor recreation during leisure periods, what duties are to be undertaken by individual staff members. They must also be briefed on any special problems which may arise – educational, social, or medical – with individual pupils. In preparation for the course, all staff should be required to acquire a working knowledge of the area around the centre, to establish local contacts if fieldwork is involved, or to participate in a scheme of theoretical and practical instruction in subjects related to the course, including conservation and safety.

In-school preparation

Classroom introduction to a residential visit is of necessity more complex and comprehensive than for a day trip because pupils have to be prepared for the residential experience as well as for activities lasting for a longer period of time.

The purpose and objectives of the course should be explained to pupils so that they understand how its practical aspects relate to the school curriculum, how they are to prepare for their experience in the classroom before departure and how it will be used in subsequent classroom studies. It is equally important that they understand the social value of a residential course: that one of the aims will be to foster a spirit of cooperation and shared experience, and that such shared experience, even if it includes some challenge and even hardship, can be rewarding and exhilarating. At the same time, they should be encouraged to consider the personal difficulties of living in a group, particularly for members who may be more shy or retiring than the average. The cultivation of a respect for individual differences of temperament and personality can be high-lighted before the visit, which may ease tensions during the stay away from home. In this context, a discussion of the balance between work and leisure activities is appropriate, and pupils can be encouraged to suggest suitable activities for leisure periods. Particular care should be taken to discuss the needs of pupils with special difficulties.

The practicalities of the visit can be raised (even with pupils who have no experience of a similar visit or the area to be visited) by, for example, asking them to 'brainstorm' the idea of all the things which could go wrong during the first twenty-four hours away – from a mislaid suitcase to a waterlogged campsite. They can then draw up lists of clothes to take, jobs to be done on arrival, methods for allotting sleeping accommodation and so on.

Thorough classroom preparation for field studies visits will reduce the amount of teaching necessary after arrival at the centre so that pupils may proceed with minimum delay to their practical activities. The interpretation and use of Ordnance Survey maps and compasses for navigation can be taught and practised in advance. Route cards, assignment cards, and questionnaires can be prepared.

Practical skills relevant to the visit may also need to be practised in advance. Expedition training may be required in preparation for mobile or static camp-craft. Initial practice can be undertaken in the skills and level of fitness needed for hill-walking, mountaineering, orienteering, rock climbing, skiing, caving, and potholing. Preparatory work for visits which will include water-based activities can be organized in the swimming baths.

All such preparatory work with pupils should emphasize safety precautions and rescue procedures appropriate to the activities to be undertaken. Pupils must know the distress signals, emergency alerts, and recall signals, and the responses required of them. Even though they are to be accompanied by a leader with a first-aid qualification, all older pupils undertaking outdoor activites should have a working knowledge of emergency first-aid procedures and be competent to undertake them. They should be warned of any particular hazards, such as cliffs or dangerous water in the locality they are to visit, and instructed never to go off alone or to swim without permission. Swimming should only be allowed with parental consent, and after taking advice from local experts on the safety of the water concerned. Pupils competent in a swimming pool may not be able to cope with open water. A qualified life-saver should be present and look-outs posted.

Attention should also be paid to conservation issues and respect should be encouraged for the natural environment and the wild life of the area to be visited. Reference should be made to the Country Code, the Mountain Code, the Outdoor Studies Code and the Water Sports Code, and the provisions of the Wildlife and Countryside Act, 1981, as appropriate.

Pupils will be eager to learn as much as possible about the

centre they will be visiting, its environment, and the activities in which they will take part. The more detailed their knowledge, the more easily they will settle in on arrival. They should be as fully informed as possible on:

- the residential accommodation and the facilities for leisure-time activities, formal or informal, shopping, correspondence, and telephoning home;
- the locality in which the centre is situated, including some details about the nearest village or town and whether it will be possible to visit local shops etc;
- the course programme and its timetabling and organization;
- the role of the resident staff and instructors, if any, and their relationship to pupils;
- centre regulations on discipline, personal behaviour, hygiene, and safety, and the rationale behind such rules;
- the school's own expectations on pupil behaviour while away, with a clearly established code of conduct (arising out of the school's own code of conduct) with specific reference to rules on smoking, alcohol, and behaviour between the sexes (if appropriate) and to the behaviour expected in unusual or stressful situations, for instance in dormitories, when unsupervised in unfamiliar surroundings, or in wild country;
- the equipment provided at the centre and its care and maintenance;
- any domestic duties which may be required;
- requirements with regard to clothing and personal equipment, with lists which itemize minimum and maximum requirements.
- Advice should be offered on books or small games suitable for leisure-time use.

At the centre

The allocation of accommodation on arrival can be undertaken most efficiently if plans of the centre and dormitory/bedroom allocation lists have been prepared in advance and duplicated for all staff members.

Exuberance amongst pupils can lead to a relatively sleepless first night. It is therefore sensible to establish and enforce a fairly rigorous bedtime discipline for pupils on the first night. This can be relaxed later when the initial excitement of being away from home has subsided.

The leader should ensure that, from the first night at the centre, staff and pupils are fully aware of fire precautions and the arrangements for evacuation of the premises. He or she should arrange for a fire drill at the earliest opportunity. Particular fire risks, such as from cooking fat or oil heaters, should be pointed out, and pupils should be firmly forbidden to smoke.

Emotional difficulties can arise even amongst older pupils if they are away from home on their own for the first time. A common manifestation is bed-wetting, which can be a cause of acute embarrassment and distress to the child concerned. Teachers should try to alleviate the bed-wetter's embarrassment, and prevent a recurrence by limiting the pupil's liquid consumption at the evening meal and ensuring adequate toilet visits. The problem is not uncommon and centres usually have a supply of rubber or plastic sheets in stock. If not, mattresses can be protected with polythene sheeting or even large plastic bags, again taking care not to embarrass the pupil over such precautions.

Homesickness can be triggered by the most trivial and apparently irrelevant incidents and can spread as a form of hysteria. It should never be dismissed as unimportant: for some children the emotional disturbance can be great enough to cause physical symptoms, and will in any case greatly spoil a pupil's ability to enjoy and play an active part in the visit. Homesickness can often be avoided or minimized by the prevention of boredom and inactivity – a build-up of homesickness amongst a group of pupils may be prevented by organizing some extra activity or challenge, possibly a treasure hunt or a barbecue. An individual pupil suffering from homesickness may be helped by being given some extra responsibility or small task to complete for the whole group. In most acute and long-lasting cases, if it is clear that the pupil is gaining no benefit from the trip and is in danger of becoming physically ill, or is disturbing the smooth running of the visit for the rest of the group, it may be advisable to consult the parents and arrange for the pupil to return home. The child should not be allowed to travel alone.

Follow-up work

It should never be forgotten that the educational value of a residential visit will be greatly enhanced by follow-up work in the classroom afterwards. The use to be made of the visit right across the curriculum should be co-ordinated by staff before departure. Even on visits without a specific fieldwork element, much can be gained by asking pupils to keep a log or diary of their experiences to be used in class later.

7

Overseas visits

Planning a visit overseas is inevitably more complex and time-consuming than a visit within the UK. But for the staff and young people involved, some of whom, even in these days of package tours, may be travelling abroad for the first time, the educational rewards can be very great. And, for teachers contemplating such a visit for the first time, there is expert help available from organizations such as the Central Bureau for Educational Visits and Exchanges, and the School Journey Association (now amalgamated with London and Educational Travel Ltd).

The first consideration should be, as with all visits, the educational purpose involved, and whether overseas travel is essential to that purpose. Meticulous preparation is needed before a party of young people can be safely taken to a country where the language, food, climate, and way of life may be unfamiliar, and where the leader and other adults with the party must accept twenty-four-hour responsibility for the whole group.

There are, of course, especially now that easier modern travel reduces risks and hardships, many educational purposes which can fully justify an overseas visit. Visits for purposes such as language learning, through an exchange with an overseas school or district, fieldwork, sporting activities or tournaments, and the sort of historical and cultural visit which can be regarded as a natural extension of classroom work, can normally be organized during termtime. Some local authorities insist that visits with a more recreational flavour, for instance a skiing trip, should be organized mainly during the school holidays, although a day or two's overlap into termtime may be permitted. It is important for teachers to consider the educational purpose of all visits. Even a skiing trip should offer opportunities for athletic and social development and entail preparation and follow-up in school if there is to be justification for a school organizing such a trip rather than a commercial travel agency doing so. Adult members of the party should always be aware that they can in no way regard themselves as 'on holiday' when they are responsible for the safety and well-being of a group of children or young people in a foreign country. There should be no question of discounted travel being available for adults who do not have any responsibility for the group.

Many schools now regularly take part in exchange arrangements with overseas schools or communities as part of their language programme. Additional help may be needed from the local authority if a town 'twinning' arrangement is involved. Continental communities often provide elaborate hospitality for 'twin' visits, which an individual school would find difficult to match without help. Where no such scheme exists, it may be worth the while of a language department which is considering augmenting pupils' learning through an overseas visit to consider whether such an exchange can be arranged. Regular exchanges, which involve pupils spending time with a foreign family, are particularly valuable as language skill increases. Many local authorities now offer financial support to students who might be excluded by the cost of such exchanges, and may offer organizational help if the exchange is made through a 'twin town' or similar arrangement.

Opportunities for social contact with young people of the country visited and of other countries can greatly enhance the value of a visit, both educationally and socially. Consideration should be given in the initial planning stages to the possibilities of arranging contact with local schools or young people on all visits overseas.

The initial planning

This is inevitably more complex than is normal for a visit within the UK, and an inspection visit to the hotels or other accommodation may not be feasible, although some tour companies can make arrangements. As a result it is more essential than ever for the group leader to make use of reputable tour organizers (if help is being sought in making travel arrangements), to seek advice from any professional or local sources which are appropriate, and if possible to contact other teachers or schools who have visited the particular area and used the same accommodation on previous occasions. A visit can be ruined by unsafe or otherwise unsatisfactory travel arrangements or accommodation, and there is no substitute for good local knowledge, if it can be obtained.

Local authorities vary in the amount of notice they require of a proposed overseas visit but a group leader should be prepared to provide a preliminary outline of the visit up to twelve months before departure, so that formal permission from the LEA and governors can be obtained in good time. The initial outline should include details of:

- the purpose of the visit
- the place to be visited
- dates of departure and return
- the composition of the party, adults, and children
- proposed levels of supervision
- the cost of the visit and whether any claim is intended for financial help towards any travel costs for students or adults
- details of insurance cover proposed
- details of any special hazards involved (canoeing, skiing, etc.)
- the method of organization – by teacher, travel agent, or other body
- the arrangements for an emergency

Governors, local authority, and the headteacher will need to be kept fully informed as plans progress.

The composition of the party, by age and sex, will determine much of the subsequent organization. When supervision is to be undertaken by non-teachers their role may have to be authorized by the LEA and they will need to be named on insurance documents. It is essential on an overseas visit, particularly if it includes a recreational element such as skiing or sightseeing, that all adults are fully informed of their responsibilities for supervision from the initial stages of planning.

The actual organization of a visit can be undertaken either by the leaders themselves or by a travel agency (some of which specialize in arrangements overseas for school parties). Consultation with colleagues in other schools or with the Central Bureau will enable leaders to locate reliable agents and tour operators. Non-profit-making organizations such as Educational Travel Ltd and the School Journey Association of London (recently amalgamated) specialize in arranging educational visits abroad, and their packages often offer the opportunity of making contact with local schools and young people in a way which a commercial agent can find difficult to arrange.

Leaders who wish to organize a tour themselves can also obtain advice from the Central Bureau on the practicalities of travel and accommodation bookings, and the special requirements of overseas planning. But whatever arrangements are made for booking the visit, the group leaders should be responsible for familiarizing themselves with the countries to be visited and with differences in law, medical arrangements, fire and safety regulations, all of which may be relevant to the health and welfare of the party. It is extremely helpful if at least one adult member of the party speaks the language of the country to be visited. If no adequate linguist is available, advice should be taken on the most useful phrase book available.

Insurance

Local authorities usually stipulate in some detail what insurance is required for an overseas visit. Further advice may also be obtained from the Central Bureau, from travel agents (who often include insurance in their package), or from professional associations. The important point for a leader to remember is that the risk of loss, accident, or medical emergency is greater, and may be more difficult to deal with, in a foreign country.

Some medical facilities are available to EEC nationals in other EEC countries, but normally only on production of Form E111, details of which are obtainable from the DHSS. The form must be completed by the parent or guardian of each individual pupil. It contains information on how to obtain emergency treatment in each EEC country.

Visits outside the EEC require separate medical insurance cover for the duration of the visit, and some tour operators and teachers consider that full medical cover is advisable within the EEC, if only to avoid financial complications when treatment is required and payment has to be made on the spot, then reclaimed later.

Supplementary cover should in any case be obtained for the additional costs of an emergency abroad, including a prolonged hospital stay, the cost of transporting sick or injured pupils and an accompanying member of staff home, and compensation in the event of severe accident. The party leader should make sure that he or she has read and is fully familiar with the insurance arrangements, that a contingency plan is made to deal with a serious emergency, particularly one involving the return of a party member to the UK, and that parents are fully informed about insurance cover and emergency arrangements.

Comprehensive insurance packages will also normally cover loss of baggage or money, and the cost of returning home early or by an alternative route or means of transport in the event of an emergency such as a strike.

Travel documents

The obtaining of appropriate passports for a group may take several months, particularly if the party is to include members who are not entitled to a full UK passport. In any case long delays sometimes occur in the issuing of passports during the spring and summer months, so procedures should be started in good time. The Central Bureau can provide detailed information on procedures, cost, and special requirements, such as visas for visits to specific countries. When passport photographs are being obtained, it is sensible for the group leader to acquire one of each member of the party, so that a complete record can be kept for use in emergencies.

There are three types of passport.

1. *A full United Kingdom passport* is valid for ten years. Application forms can be obtained from a main post office, but the processing may take at least four weeks. It is a sensible investment for students over the age of 14 who may intend to travel abroad again in the near future.
2. *A British visitor's passport* is valid for twelve months, and is obtainable direct from a main post office. It is only valid for travel in certain Western European countries for visits of not more than three months.
3. *A collective passport* for the whole or part of the group can be issued to approved parties of UK nationals who are under 18 and travelling in the charge of a responsible leader. Non-UK nationals and existing holders of a full UK passport cannot be included on a group passport. The leader of a group using a collective passport must hold a full UK passport. Applications must be accompanied by a supporting letter from the headteacher, local authority, or governors. Some countries impose their own restrictions on the use of collective passports and on who may be included. The application to the passport office should include details of the countries to be visited, the number of pupils involved, how many of them will be 16 or over on re-entry to the UK, and the country of birth of any members of the group born outside the UK but holding a UK passport. Members of the party over 16 must also carry an identity card with a photograph.

If the group includes pupils whose nationality or immigration status or entitlement to a British passport is in doubt, it would be wise to make very early general enquiries of the Foreign and Commonwealth Office concerning the requirements of the Immigration Act and the right of re-entry to the UK. The British Nationality Act of 1981 may have created difficulties in respect of the pupils concerned which extend to the use of collective and visitor's passports. In individual cases of doubt, further authoritative advice can be obtained from the Joint Council for the Welfare of Immigrants (JCWI).

Leaders should avoid creating worries and difficulties for children and their families by casting doubt upon individuals' immigration, nationality, or 'settled' status. In particular, approaches should not be made to the Home Office about individuals without first seeking advice from the JCWI. In some cases, group leaders may even wish to reconsider making an overseas journey if the effect of these difficulties discriminates against some pupils in the school.

Members of a group travelling on a collective passport are expected to travel and stay together. If in an emergency members of the group need to travel separately, then individual travel documents have to be obtained from the British Consulate. Some countries require a copy of the collective passport to be lodged at the frontier and extra copies of the document should be carried by the leader for this purpose.

Until recently it was possible to make day trips to Holland, Belgium, and France using only an identity card. For trips to France the regulations have now been changed and an excursion document valid for one month is required.

Student cards are a valuable additional document for any young people eligible to use them. The International Student/Scholar Identity Card is available to students over 14. Further information on these cards is available from the Central Bureau; they carry with them concessions on fares, museum entrance costs, and so on.

Some leaders provide all party members with a card in the language of the country to be visited with a simple message asking for help, and including details of the hotel or centre of residence, and telephone numbers.

Health and welfare

It is particularly important when travelling abroad to obtain in advance full details of any medical conditions which may require treatment on the journey or while abroad, e.g. allergies, epilepsy, asthma, serious travel-sickness. A prompt-list is helpful to ensure that nothing significant is forgotten. Girls should be asked to bring adequate supplies with them to deal with menstrual periods.

One party leader should be qualified in basic first aid and carry a first-aid kit and simple medical supplies. Pupils should be advised not to drink tap water unless the leader has established that it is safe to do so. Group members taking medication should provide full information in writing on exactly what is prescribed, and how often it must be administered. One adult in the party should take responsibility for all members requiring regular medication. Some medical problems may require discussion with a parent before a child is accepted as a member of the group.

There is advice on vaccination and injection requirements for certain countries and on the steps to be taken by anyone bitten by an animal, etc., in the DHSS leaflet SA35.

Consent forms should contain a clause giving advance permission for urgent medical treatment in the event of accident or injury, or vaccination if there has been a risk of infection, in case parents cannot be contacted personally.

Foreign currency

Major expenses for travel and accommodation will have in most cases been met before a party leaves. However, the group leader will require funds to meet travel expenses for the group in transit. Arrangements to obtain traveller's cheques and some currency should be made in good time through the bank handling the special account for the visit.

Pupils should have a maximum amount of pocket-money specified. If the group is travelling on a collective passport this money will have to be held by the group leader and accounted for on entering the country concerned. In any event, many group leaders prefer to take charge of pocket-money for pupils, organize the exchange into the appropriate foreign currency, and act as a pocket-money 'bank' during the visit so that spending is sensibly spread out. This requires careful accounting by teachers on the pupils' behalf. Pupils should be advised in advance of the currency they will be using and given a rough rate of exchange so that they are not confused when they attempt to shop.

Baggage

It is in the interests of the whole group that the amount of luggage taken should be no more than any group member can carry easily while transferring from train or coach to plane or ferry. Light suitcases pack more easily into restricted luggage space than rucksacks. Labels should be provided for outward and inward journeys and advice given on suitable clothing, especially if the visit is to anywhere unusually hot or cold. It is worth recommending pupils to attach a contents list to the inside of their suitcase, to be checked off before the return journey. Group members should be restricted to one suitcase and a shoulder bag or small hold-all for use on the journey. All articles should be clearly labelled. Group members should be warned about the restricted list of items which can be taken on board an aircraft or packed in baggage to be carried in the hold.

Customs regulations

Adult duty-free allowances are not applicable to young people under 17, and this should be made clear to all members of the party before they have access to duty-free shops at ports or airports. Copies of the full regulations are available at ports and airports and the group should be warned that some articles, for instance flick knives and dangerous souvenirs, will be confiscated at ports and airports of entry. Pupils will have bought souvenirs or presents, and it will speed up customs clearance if they, or the group leader, can present a list of purchases to officers at the port or airport.

En route

Any school visit abroad may include some young people who have never been out of the UK before, and special consideration should be given to their welfare. They are more likely than more seasoned travellers to be nervous of air travel, worried about the possibility of travel-sickness, and confused or worried by their new environment. Careful planning by the leader and other adults can ensure that the inward and outward journeys are as trouble-free and enjoyable as possible. Pupils should be specifically instructed on what to expect at air- and sea-ports, the procedures to be followed going through passport control and customs, and how to behave on ferries and aircraft. On a long journey they should be told what food and drink to carry and what it may be possible to buy – at what price – on the journey. They should be warned that snacks and soft drinks may be more expensive abroad than in the UK.

Group travel documents entail keeping the group together at times when tickets may have to be checked. Group members may need to carry individual landing tickets or, on trains, 'contremarques' as evidence of their membership of the group. Loss of such documents may cost the group time and money.

All group members should be advised of the additional road safety hazards when traffic moves on the opposite side of the road, and that in some countries 'jay-walking' is prohibited and an instant fine imposed, so pedestrian crossings must be used.

If a mini-bus is being used local authority advice should be sought on regulations governing its use abroad, and a motoring organization should be consulted about regulations governing mini-bus use in the countries to be visited, licence requirement, insurance, tachograph requirements and traffic regulations.

Codes of conduct

Young people travelling in groups abroad are in a particular way representative of their country. Bad behaviour in public, on ferries, at ports, or in the street, is particularly noticeable and damages the image of Britain as well as that of the school. In some ways groups of young people are a target for trouble: they are attractive to drug-pushers, and for that reason particularly likely to be stopped, interviewed, and even searched by the police.

Young people old enough to be taken on an overseas visit are also old enough to recognize the damage which has been done to Britain's reputation by young people abroad in recent years, and should be clearly reminded of their responsibility to behave courteously and sensibly while away from home. It is extremely useful if at least one adult member of the party has a good working knowledge of the language of the country being visited.

Any code of conduct should arise naturally out of what is expected at school, but it is probably necessary to spell out exactly what is and is not permitted on a visit, particularly to a strange country, depending on the age of the party members. Leaders should familiarize themselves with the local law on matter such as consumption of alcohol and drugs, in case of emergency, but should in any case consider an absolute prohibition on smoking, alcohol, pornography and any other unusual temptations which may come the way of members of the party in a strange country. Rules for the duration of the visit should be negotiated with parents and young people. Hotels will usually cooperate by refusing to serve alcohol to young people if they are requested to do so. School parties are especially notorious for rowdy behaviour on ferries so strict guidelines should be laid down as to what is permissible throughout the journey. Pupils' free time, particularly in the evenings, should be limited and supervision provided at all times. Pupils should not be left unsupervised in hotels or residences at night. One teacher should always remain on duty. Pupils should not leave the main group at all without permission, and always in groups, not alone. Pupils should not climb, ski, or swim without permission and supervision. Sensible rules on rest and bedtimes should be agreed with the whole party before departure.

On a visit to a strange country, and schools are increasingly moving further and further afield, the level of supervision cannot be too careful.

Communication with home

Just as some pupils may be anxious about a long visit, so too parents may worry about children on a first trip abroad. The leader should take on, or delegate, the responsibility of ensuring that all members of the party send a postcard or make a telephone call, notifying their parents of their safe arrival, and should also facilitate any other communication, by letter or telephone, which parents may be expecting. The group leader should ensure that adults in the party understand how to use the local telephone system, and precisely what they should do in an emergency in the absence of the group leader. But young people should not expect to make long-distance calls at the expense of families with whom they may be staying.

A foolproof system of contact with the school and all parents should have been arranged before departure, and details of this should be held by the leader at all times in case of emergency.

Particular care should be taken on an exchange visit to ensure that young people staying with a strange family for any length of time do not become homesick. It is sometimes difficult to recognize the symptoms, and the programme should be arranged so that pupils do not spend too long alone with families in circumstances where they might not be able to communicate their feelings or worries easily. Arrangements should always be made for pupils to contact someone locally who speaks fluent English with whom it is possible to discuss problems which may arise during the course of an exchange.

Home–school liaison

A meeting with families to estimate likely interest in the visit should be organized as soon as initial plans have been finalized. At this stage some estimate of the likely cost should be given to parents, and arrangements proposed for payment by instalment over the months leading up to the visit.

Parents should be kept fully informed and involved as plans become firmer, and should be provided with information of location, including the full address and telephone number of hotels, the departure and arrival times for outward and inward journeys, methods of travel, the names of the accompanying adults, details of the clothing and equipment required, consent forms, and confirmation of cost as early as possible. Parents will also wish to know the levels of supervision proposed during pupils' free time, as well as during activity periods.

From parents, the group leader will require addresses and telephone numbers (including, if applicable, holiday addresses) while the party is away, and consent forms appropriately signed. Teachers will have to consider very carefully whether they are willing to be responsible abroad for a pupil whose parents, on grounds of conscience, will not sign a consent form for emergency medical treatment. Schools do have the right to refuse to take pupils on a visit.

Pupil preparation

Part of the educational value of any visit abroad must be the contact with another culture and language, possibly for the first time. Even on a visit which is largely recreational in character, it is important for pupils to have spent some time learning about the country to be visited, its history and traditions, and its language.

For many young people the most immediate impact of a different culture will come at the dining table, and some introduction to the sort of food which can be expected is essential.

83

Pupils should also be introduced to the local currency and, if the language concerned is not one with which they are already familiar, some simple phrases to assist them in shops can be provided.

In—school liaison

An official contact at home who can be reached by telephone day and night should be available for the whole duration of the visit. The contact should have the names, addresses, and telephone numbers of the parents/guardians of all members of the party and the school and home telephone number of the headteacher and a local authority contact, full details of the group's itinerary, accommodation, and telephone numbers, the name and address of the travel agent or tour company and, if applicable, the telephone number for use in emergency provided under the local authority's insurance arrangements. The contact should be both willing and able to respond to an emergency at all times during the visit, and able to relay any necessary information about delays, illness, medical treatment, and arrangements for repatriation or for the flying out of relatives to visit a sick or injured member of the party. The contact should also have the name and address and telephone number of consular officials in the country to be visited, which information should also be carried by the group leader.

8

School and community activities

An increasing number of schools now involve older pupils in visits to industrial and commercial enterprises as a means of broadening their experience by observation, or on a longer term basis to offer them actual experience of a working environment. Other schools ask pupils in fifth- and sixth-year groups to take part in community activities which may involve assisting in a range of worthwhile enterprises include the local playgroup, hospitals for the mentally ill and handicapped, adventure playgrounds, and the homes of individual old people who need help with decorating or gardening.

There are clear educational advantages to young people in this sort of direct experience of local industry and the community. But the school remains responsible for pupils' welfare and safety when they are off the premises, even if they are beyond statutory school-leaving age.

Industrial visits to relatively hazardous sites such as quarries and factories are an established tradition and one during which supervision of small groups of pupils may have to be passed from the group leader to staff members at the enterprise concerned. The safety record of this sort of visit is good, but leaders should always remember that the industrial environment is hazardous, and that proper preparation and precautions are essential when planning such a visit.

Community activities may involve less obvious hazard, but pupils should be equally carefully prepared for situations in which individual supervision may very well be impossible and during which they may have to take responsibility not only for themselves but for younger, older, or less competent people than themselves. In either an industrial or a community situation, one of the primary educational aims will be to encourage young people's own self-discipline and sense of personal responsibility.

In particular there should be careful preparation in the classroom for the visit or series of visits proposed. The visits may be organized to foster pupils' understanding of the community in which they live and will work, and in many cases to allow them to gain practical experience of that work or involvement. Firsthand experience is valuable in helping young people see how the adult world organizes itself, how adult relationships at work or in institutions function, and how adults and contemporaries experience a life which may be very different from that of the pupils themselves. The purpose of other visits may be to allow pupils to develop powers of observation and empathy and to foster particular social and technical skills. Aims and objectives should always be discussed in advance and evaluated afterwards.

All these objectives imply a high degree of participation and involvement by the pupils, often over an extended period. Discussion of aims and objectives with pupils should include discussion of the fact that teacher supervision will not be available – nor even desirable – on some visits of this kind, and that the development of personal responsibility for safety may be paramount in some of the situations to be experienced. Discussion can focus on the hazards which may be encountered, and how they can be minimized by the individual pupil, e.g. in an industrial environment, the absolute necessity to wear safety clothing and equipment and obey safety regulations; in a domestic environment such as an old person's home, the need to remember basic safety rules when dealing with fire and ladders.

There are useful videos available on community work and activities, and small group discussion may be invaluable in enabling young people to prepare for their activities and, a very important aspect, for their own emotional response to what may be unusual and even stressful situations. A feeling of inadequacy can be minimized if young people are helped to contribute positively to working out new activities for the people they may be intending to help in some way.

Industrial and work experience visits

Pupils under the statutory school-leaving age are allowed to participate in work experience schemes only during their last year at school. Such schemes are regulated by the local authority and may be organized by individual schools or centrally through the careers service, or through such schemes as Trident. The local authority regulations must be strictly followed and there are time limits on how long pupils may work.

Work experience is regulated by the Education (Work Experience) Act 1973 amplified by the DES Circular 7/74, which was issued to local authorities for guidance on how work experience should be regulated and monitored. Some local authorities also issue their own guidelines on work experience, so leaders should consult their local authority before embarking on any work experience scheme.

Initial contact with a firm willing to allow a visit to its premises, or work experience there, may be made personally, through the local authority careers service or one of the educational and/or industrial agencies such as SCIP, UBI, Trident etc. (see appendix). Early contact with a named person responsible for the organization of the visit or visits is essential. The teacher needs reassurance that the premises comply with the regulations made under the Health and Safety at Work Act 1974 and related legislation, and that pupils will be properly supervised at all times while on the premises. The Act is backed up by codes of practice which detail how employers can fulfil their obligations under the Act, but experienced work experience organizers warn that some employers only pay lip service, at best, to health and safety requirements, and that careful visiting of the premises, and discussion of the safety aspects of pupils' experience is essential before any work experience scheme is confirmed. Teachers in any doubt about safety matters on non-school premises should consult the local authority, headteacher, and, if necessary, the Health and Safety Executive.

It may also be necessary, in the interests of safety (and of course in complete confidentiality) to provide the manager or supervisor with information about the pupils who will be taking part in the activity, if the information has any bearing on their health and safety while away from school.

There should be a clear agreement on supervision between the teacher in charge and the workplace personnel involved. A leader can only delegate responsibility to a guide or supervisor if sure that such a person is fully competent and understands the role and its responsibilities.

Checks should be made to ensure that no pupil is exposed to conditions or work for which he or she is medically unsuited. The activities to be undertaken by any member of a group should in any case be individually determined by the teacher and industrial supervisor in consultation. Some pupils, for instance those suffering from asthma or eczema or from colour blindness, may be vulnerable to particular industrial hazards; work may be too strenuous for others, or may demand skills they do not have. The advice of the school doctor may be needed on the activities to be expected of individual pupils, as well as a party as a whole.

Care should also be taken to ensure that pupils are not exposed to embarrassment or discrimination on a work experience placement on the grounds of their race, sex, or ability level. Such issues should be discussed with potential employers before a pupil is offered a placement. And care should be taken to ensure that pupils on work experience are not exploited in any way by their employers, particularly in industries like catering which employ large numbers of young people on a casual or part-time basis.

Pupils should be fully briefed about the purpose of their visit or visits, potential dangers, first aid and safety regulations, and first aid procedures. The firm should confirm that all necessary protective clothing and equipment will be available to pupils. Maximum benefit from a visit or a period of work experience can only be expected if there has been full classroom preparation and discussion, and if there is follow-up afterwards. Industrial supervisors of pupils on work experience schemes are often asked to produce a report on the pupil performance after the work experience has finished. Careful evaluation is essential if pupils are to gain maximum benefit from an experience which is intended to enable them to conclude that they either do or do not feel that an area of work suits them. The School Curriculum Industry Partnership (SCIP) produces useful publications giving practical advice to teachers on work experience, shadowing, and simulation.

Parents should be consulted fully about all industrial visits and work experience placements, given full details about the objectives, and what the pupil will be doing while away from school. Their consent should be sought in writing.

Adequate insurance arrangements should be made to cover the period of the visit or visits. The local authority itself may have a scheme to cover such activities but, in any case, should be consulted before firm plans are made. A number of institutions and firms ask for an indemnity against accidents or damage caused by visitors who cannot be held to be in their employment. Pupils on work experience visits must not be paid and are not covered by the National Insurance (Industrial Injuries) Act, so it is vital that school, parents, industrial supervisor and local authority are satisfied with the insurance arrangements in force. The DES advises schools and local authorities to make sure that their own insurance arrangements are adequate to meet any liabilities arising from an accident to a pupil engaged in work experience. Insurance arrangements should be clearly explained to parents in advance.

Community activities

Many schools now organize community service activities for older pupils which take pupils out of school into working environments such as hospitals or schools, into private homes, to adventure playgrounds, or to other outdoor sites where useful work is to be done. The organizer of such activities carries the same responsibility as a work experience organizer for visiting the sites where pupils will be taking part in activities, and defining clearly both to the pupils and to other adults involved in their supervision, or to members of the public who may benefit from their services, exactly what their role is to be, and what they may and may not do. It is also important to clarify with the local authority and the headteacher whether they are fully covered by the local authority's insurance. Parents should be fully informed of exactly what work is to be undertaken, and what insurance cover is provided.

For pupils to gain the full educational benefit from community activities preparation and follow-up in the classroom should be just as thorough as for any other out-of-school visit, and pupils themselves should be encouraged to take part in the planning and preparation of projects, and in their evaluation. It is often helpful to invite community supervisors into school to meet pupils, discuss activities and problems and reinforce the relationship between the school and the receiving institutions. Supervisors should be asked to report back to the school if any activity involving pupils appears to them to be unsafe, or if there are any difficulties over the acceptability of certain pupils to their clients on grounds of race or sex. Similarly pupils should be asked to report immediately any personal difficulties they may encounter while on a community placement.

9

Adventurous activities

Most secondary schools organize some out-of-school activities in which an inherent risk forms an integral part of the activity and cannot be eliminated without detracting from the nature and quality of the activity itself. Indeed preparing and enabling young people to cope with an element of risk is part of the educational purpose of some activities, in particular those leading to qualifications such as the Duke of Edinburgh's Award.

Mountain and moorland areas, coastal and inland waterways attract young people seeking challenge and adventure and the development of new outdoor skills. In activities of this sort it is often the environment itself which offers a particular challenge to the group leader and other members of the party, and the environment can be influenced by factors other than the merely geographical, although *they* can be formidable enough. Weather conditions, changes in temperature, in wind strength and direction, and in the amount of rainfall, snow, or cloud cover can drastically alter the nature of a locality very swiftly and create additional hazards. Of course hazardous situations can arise in the course of any activity, but there are gradations, and an accident in remote country or on a mountainside carries with it additional difficulties which need to be recognized. It should be the aim of leaders of out-of-school activities of this type to ensure that they and their pupils are thoroughly prepared both for the inherent risk of the activity itself, and for dealing competently and with confidence with unexpected danger in a possibly wild and remote environment. Essential initial reading for teachers proposing to organize adventurous activities for young people is *Safety in Outdoor Pursuits*, DES Safety Series No.1, published by HMSO. (See appendix for details of CCPR.) They should also read the safety advice of the governing bodies of the sports or activities concerned.

Leadership

Trained and experienced leadership is essential for the organization of out-of-school activities which are inherently hazardous or which will take place in potentially hazardous areas. Accidents most frequently occur through inadequate leadership resulting in the underestimation of hazards and difficulties, inappropriate clothing or equipment or lack of preparation. Qualifications for leaders of out-of-school activities are now offered by many of the sporting and outdoor activity bodies concerned, and by the Central Council of Physical Recreation. The basic qualification for leaders of outdoor activities is now provided by the CCPR, in conjunction with the DES and the governing bodies of sports and other national organizations. The Community Sports Leadership Training Programme leads to the Basic Expedition Training Award (BETA), which gives a thorough grounding in camping, navigation, care of oneself and others, and of the countryside, etc. without the specialized content of the more advanced Mountain-walking Leader Training Board awards. Some local authorities also organize their own training schemes.

But while training and experience are essential, they do not guarantee safety, which in the end only comes from constant vigilance and careful preparation to meet any hazard. In particular the leader should be physically fit, and have all the necessary skills, techniques, and experience to be able to cope with children of the age group involved, with the particular sport or activity, and with the location of the visit, at the time of year it is being organized. Open and wild country in the winter is very different from the same terrain in summertime. The selection of other adults to accompany the trip is also vital to safety: activities may well be organized on a group basis and every adult taking a supervisory role should be sufficiently experienced for the task, and able to inspire the confidence of a group under what may be difficult conditions. A clear chain of command should be established for all circumstances of the visit.

The leader of an activity which is inherently hazardous should be able to:

1. Identify and understand all the potential risks involved and make a decision in advance about how to deal with each particular risk.
2. Eliminate or reduce each risk by providing extra supervision and close assistance, offering training or instruction, and providing appropriate equipment and protective clothing.
3. Plan for the possibility of foreseen dangers arising, while remaining flexible enough to deal with unexpected hazards.
4. Ensure that all members of the party thoroughly understand the nature of the hazards involved and the measures to be taken to minimize them.

The leader should in particular take responsibility for ensuring that all those taking a supervisory role during the activity have access to the available advice and codes of conduct prepared by the expert bodies of the sport or activity concerned. Expert advice should be provided not only on sports and activities but also on ancillary matters such as camping, route-finding, and fire and first aid precautions. (See Appendix for a full list of advisory codes and booklets.)

Training should extend to all adults who take part in a visit, and to the young people themselves, who should if possible be familiarized with the activities to be undertaken and the locality and terrain to be visited. Active preparation and training may involve young people in the use of dry ski slopes, ice rinks, climbing walls, cross-country work, camping and cooking experience in and around school or college, practice in the use of maps and compasses, first aid and general fitness training.

Preparation for a visit

Most local authorities have specific procedures for the granting of permission for pupils and young people to take part in adventurous activities. Some LEAs impose a total ban on certain activities, such as hang-gliding, where they consider the risk factor outweighs the educational advantage. With regard to adventurous activities, group leaders should be aware that stringent local authority regulations apply over such things as leadership qualifications, insurance, adult–pupil ratios, and consents. They should clear their proposed visit or activity with the headteacher, governors, and local authority before publicizing it to pupils and parents.

In preparing for a visit there is no substitute for training, experience, a detailed knowledge of the activities proposed and locality to be visited, and close attention to the guides and codes prepared by the specialist organizations. Nor is there space in a general guide of this kind to provide detailed guidance on the organization of adventurous activities. Specialist guidance is needed and is available. However, the following check-list may be of help to leaders preparing for a range of outdoor activities of an adventurous kind.

BETA Award Scheme check-list

1. Are all adults properly qualified and experienced for all the activities to be undertaken? (This includes instructors at any activities centre to be used.)
2. Is additional training for adults advisable and available?
3. Has a preliminary visit been arranged to the site to be used and terrain to be covered in activities away from base, and are the leaders familiar with the location of telephones, doctor, hospital, police, coastguard, and mountain rescue organization if needed in case of emergency?
4. Has all suitable advisory material (including codes of practice) been obtained in good time for all who will need it?

5. Are all supervising adults familiar with the younger members of the party, their skills, and their limitations?

6. Have parents been kept fully informed about the nature of the visit and the activities to be undertaken, the levels of supervision and qualifications of supervisors for particular activities? And have all permissions from parents been obtained according to local authority guidelines?

7. Has insurance cover been checked, and details provided for parents?

8. Have all pupils been fully involved in preparation, through discussion and practical activities, for the visit and related activities?

9. Have check-lists been prepared for all members of the party with regard to what they must provide in the way of equipment and clothing?

10. Do members of the party have the necessary first aid and/or life-saving experience, and are they able to deal with casualties in need of rescuscitation, to recognize the symptoms of exhaustion or exposure and to take appropriate measures to combat them?

11. Has the party been fully briefed on particular hazards associated with the visit: e.g. sanitation and food preparation routines when camping, fire drills, safety procedures in open country in the event of accident or sudden weather deterioration, safety procedures for water sports, caving, abseiling, etc.?

12. Have clear guidelines been drawn up for the routines necessary for the party's safety, e.g. the lodging of route cards, estimated times of arrival, etc., and for the procedures to be followed by all party members in an emergency on land or water?

13. Is all necessary equipment and clothing available on site, and has it been checked for conformity to appropriate quality and safety standards? (e.g. ropes, canoes, life-jackets, helmets, survival bags, etc.)

14. Are emergency links with the school or college and parents clearly laid down and available to all who may need them?

15. Have medical and fitness checks been made to ensure that all members of the party are capable of the activities to be undertaken, such as the checking of medical records,

swimming ability for water sports, etc.?

16. Does the entire party understand that safety checks and codes of conduct will be rigorously enforced at all times in the interests of the safety of the party as a whole?

17. Do all members of the party understand the lines of command which will apply away from base and during small group activities?

18. Has there been a thorough programme of preparation, including practice where applicable, covering routes, navigation, the nature of activities proposed, the nature of the terrain or water, weather conditions, emergency procedures, and the clothing and equipment required by each individual?

Appendix
Useful
publications and addresses

SCDC is funded for curriculum development work in England and Wales. The information in the book relates to that context although the general safety messages have an obvious wider significance.

The material under each heading is organized in the order *Books and leaflets etc.*, *Useful addresses*, and (where such exist) *Codes of practice.*

Some books listed are out of print but will probably still be available in libraries. An asterisk before an organization indicates that it is a governing body.

General

Books and leaflets

Assistant Masters and Mistresses Association (September 1986) *The School Minibus and the Law*, London: AMMA.
   (1987) *Out of School* (3rd edn), London: AMMA.
Barrell, G.R. and Partington, J. (1985) *Teachers and the Law* (6th edition), London: Methuen.
Buckinghamshire County Council (1985) *School Visit to Cornwall by Stoke Poges County Middle School, May 1985*, Report of Chief Education Officer (Garrett Report), Buckinghamshire County Council.
Carter, F. (1987) *Educational Visits and Journeys*, NFER for EMIE.

Central Council of Physical Recreation (n.d.) *Community Sports Leaders Award Scheme*, London: CCPR.
Chartered Institute of Public Finance and Accountancy (1980) *VAT Treatment of Organized School Visits: Modified Guidance from Customs and Excise*, London: CIPFA.
The Council for Environmental Education (1986) *The Good Stay Guide*, Shaftesbury: Broadcast Books.
Introductory Activities into the Environment. Available from CEE at the University of Reading.
Department of Education and Science (1983) *Learning Out of Doors: An HMI Survey of Outdoor Education and Short-stay Residential Experience*, London: HMSO.
Dring, T. and Collins, M. (1986) *An Introduction to Basic Minibus Driving*, Birmingham: The Royal Society for the Prevention of Accidents.
Girl Guides Association (1986) *The Outdoor Manual*, London: Girl Guides Association.
The Head's Legal Guide (periodically updated) Section 4: 'External dealings', New Maldon: Croner Publications.
Keay W. (1987) *Duke of Edinburgh's Award Expedition Guide*. Duke of Edinburgh's Award Scheme.
Mortlock, C. (1984) *The Adventure Alternative*, Cicerone Press (Harmany Hall, Milnthorpe, Cumbria LA7 7QE).
National Association of Head Teachers (August 1984) *Council Memorandum on Supervision*, London: NAHT.
National Union of Teachers (1986) *Beyond the Classroom: Guidance from the National Union of Teachers on School Visits and Journeys*, London: NUT.
Nature Conservancy Council (1982) *Wildlife, the Law and You*, Peterborough: Nature Conservancy Council.

Useful addresses

The Association of British Travel Agents Ltd, 55–7 Newman Street, London W1P 4AN. Tel. 01-637 2444.
The Association of Wardens of Outdoor Education Centres, Fellside Centre, Caldbeck, Cumbria CA7 8HA. Tel. 0699 3307.
British Activity Holiday Association, P.O. Box 99, Tunbridge Wells, Kent TN1 2EL. Tel. 0892 49868.
British Association of Advisers and Lecturers in Physical Education. Secretary: Mr J. Bailey, Adviser for Physical Education, Education Department, County Hall, Glenfield, Leics LE3 8RF. Tel. 0533 317772.
The Central Bureau, Seymour Mews House, Seymour Mews,

London W1H 9PC. Tel. 01–486 5101.

The Central Council for Physical Recreation, Francis House, Francis Street, London SW1P 1DE. Tel. 01–828 3163/4.

Commonwealth Youth Exchange Council, 18 Fleet Street, London EC4Y 1AA.

Consumers Association, 14 Buckingham Street, London WC2N 6DS. Tel. 01–839 1222.

The Council for Environmental Education, School of Education, University of Reading, London Road, Reading RG1 5AQ. Tel. 0734 875234.

*The Countrywide Holiday Association, Birch Heys, Cromwell Range, Manchester M14 6HU. Tel. 061–225 1000.

English Heritage, Education Department, 15 Great Marlborough Street, London W1V 1AF. Tel. 01–734 6010.

*The Girl Guides Association, 17–19 Buckingham Palace Road, London SW1W 0PT. Tel. 01–834 6242.

National Association for Environmental Education, West Midlands College of Higher Education, Gorway, Walsall, West Midlands WS1 3BD. Tel. 0922 31200.

National Association for Outdoor Education, Doncaster Metropolitan Institute of Higher Education, High Melton, Doncaster DN5 7SZ. Tel. 0709 582427.

National Panel of Advisers in Outdoor Education, Education Department, 5 Portland Square, Carlisle CA1 1PU.

National Union of Students, 461 Holloway Road, N7 6LJ. Tel. 01–272 8900.

National Youth Bureau, 17–23 Albion Street, Leicester LE1 6GD. Tel. 0533 554775.

Physical Education Association, 162 Kings Cross Road, London WC1X 9DH. Tel. 01–278 9311.

The Royal Society for the Prevention of Accidents (RoSPA), Cannon House, The Priory Queensway, Birmingham B4 6BS. Tel. 021–200 2461.

The School Journey Association of London, 48 Cavendish Road, Clapham South, London SW12 0GD. Tel. 01–673 4849.

*The Scout Association, Baden-Powell House, 65 Queen's Gate, London SW7 5JS. Tel. 01–584 7030.

The Sports Council, 16 Upper Woburn Place, London WC1H 0QP. Tel. 01–388 1277.

Youth Exchange Centre, Seymour Mews House, Seymour Mews, London W14 9PE. Tel. 01–486 5101.

*Youth Hostels Association, Trevelyan House, 8 St Stephen's Hill, St Albans, Herts AL1 2DY. Tel. 0727 55215.

*Youth Hostels Association of Scotland, 7 Glebe Crescent, Sterling FK8 2JA. Tel. 0786 72821.
*Youth Hostels Association of Northern Ireland, 56 Bradbury Place, Belfast BL7. Tel. 0232 224733.

Health, safety, and first aid

Publications and organizations relating to specific activities are listed in the appropriate sections.

Books and leaflets

Balchin, R.G.A. (Director General, St John Ambulance) (1984) *Emergency Aid in Schools*, Reading: Hills & Lacey.
British Association of Advisers and Lecturers in Physical Education (1985) *Safe Practice in Physical Education* (revised edition), Leicester: BAALPE.
British Red Cross Society (1985) *Motorists' First Aid*, London: Dorling Kindersley, in association with the British Red Cross Society.
(1985) *Pocket First Aid*, London: Dorling Kindersley, in association with the British Red Cross Society.
(1984) *Practical First Aid*, London: Dorling Kindersley, in association with the British Red Cross Society.
Department of Education and Science (1978) *Safety in Physical Education* (revised edition) London: HMSO.
(1979) *Safety in Outdoor Pursuits*, Safety Series 1, London: HMSO.
(1986) *Children at School and Problems Related to AIDS*, London: HMSO.
(1987) *AIDS, Some Questions and Answers. Facts for Teachers, Lecturers and Youth Workers*, London: HMSO.
Department of Transport (1987) *Highway Code*, London: HMSO. *Safety on Sponsored Walks*, London: HMSO.
Hannam, P. (1987) *Simply Safe: Guidelines on Basic Health and Safety at Work*, Bristol: Youth Education Service Publications.
Health Education Authority (n.d.) *Minor Illness: How to Treat it in the Home*, London: HEA.
Health Education Authority Project (1988) *Safety*, Health Education in Initial Teacher Education, Unit 6, Health Education Unit, University of Southampton.
Molloy, C.C. (for St John Ambulance) (1987) *Essentials of First Aid*, Reading: Hills & Lacey.

Appendix

National Association for Outdoor Education (1984) *Safety Principles in Outdoor Education*, Doncaster: National Association for Outdoor Education.

National Union of Teachers (n.d.) *Acquired Immune Deficiency Syndrome*, Health and Safety in Schools No. 7, London: NUT.

RoSPA (1985) *Out and About: Organizing School Trips*, Birmingham: RoSPA.

The Royal Society for the Prevention of Accidents Safety Education Department, road safety education materials, Birmingham: RoSPA.

St John Ambulance Association, St Andrew's Ambulance Association, and the British Red Cross Society (1987) *First Aid Manual: Emergency Procedures for Everyone at Home, at Work or at Leisure*, London: Dorling Kindersley.

Useful addresses

The British Red Cross Society, 9 Grosvenor Crescent, London SW1X 7EJ. Tel. 01-235 5454.

British Safety Council, 62 Chancellors Road, London W6 9RS. Tel. 01-741 1231.

Child Accident Prevention Trust, 75 Portland Place, London W1N 3AL. Tel. 01-636 2545.

Fire Protection Association, 140 Aldersgate Street, London EC1A 4HX. Tel. 01-606 3757.

Health and Safety Commission, Baynards House, 1 Chepstow Place, Westbourne Grove, London W2 4TF. Tel. 01-229 3456.

Health Education Authority, 78 New Oxford Street, London WC1A 1AH. Tel. 01-631 0930.

Safety Education Department, The Royal Society for the Prevention of Accidents, Cannon House, The Priory, Queensway, Birmingham B4 6BS. Tel. 021-200 2461.

*St Andrew's Ambulance Association, Milton Street, Glasgow. Tel. 041 332 4031.

*St John Ambulance, 1 Grosvenor Crescent, London SW1X 7EF. Tel. 01-235 5231.

Youth Education Service, 14 Frederick Place, Bristol BS8 1AS.

Health and Safety Executive local offices

1. *South:* Priestley House, Priestley Road, Basingstoke RG24 9NW. Tel. 0256 473181.
2. *South East:* 3 East Grinstead House, London Road, East Grinstead, West Sussex RH19 1RR. Tel. 0342 26922.

3. *South West:* Inter City House, Mitchell Lane, Bristol BS1 6AN. Tel. 0272 290681.

4. *London North:* Maritime House, 1 Linton Road, Barking, Essex, IG11 8HF. Tel. 01-594 5522. (Merger of area offices 4 and 5.)

5. *London South:* 1 Long Lane, London SE1 4PG. Tel. 01-407 8911.

6. *East Anglia:* 39 Baddow Road, Chelmsford, Essex CM2 0HL. Tel. 0245 84661.

7. *Northern Home Counties:* 14 Cardiff Road, Luton, Bedfordshire LU1 1PP. Tel. 0582 34121.

8. *East Midlands:* Belgrave House, 1 Greyfriars, Northampton NN1 2BS. Tel. 0604 21233.

9. *West Midlands:* McLaren Buildings, 2 Masshouse Circus, Queensway, Birmingham B4 7NP. Tel. 021-236 5080.

10. *Wales:*Brunel House, 2 Fitzalan Road, Cardiff CF2 1SH. Tel. 0222 497777.

11. *Marches:* The Marches House, Midway, Newcastle-under-Lyme, Staffordshire ST5 1DT. Tel. 0782 610181.

12. *North Midlands:* Birkbeck House, Trinity Square, Nottingham NG1 4AU. Tel. 0602 470712.

13. *South Yorkshire:* Sovereign House, 40 Silver Street, Sheffield S1 2ES. Tel. 0742 739081.

14. *West and North Yorks:* 8 St Paul's Street, Leeds LS1 2LE. Tel. 0532 446191.

15. *Greater Manchester:* Quay House, Quay Street, Manchester M3 3JB. Tel. 061-831 7111.

16. *Merseyside:* The Triad, Stanley Road, Bootle L20 3PG. Tel. 051-922 7211.

17. *North West:* Victoria House, Ormskirk Road, Preston PR1 1HH. Tel. 00772 59321.

18. *North East:* Arden House, Regent Centre, Regent Farm Road, Gosforth, Newcastle-upon-Tyne NE3 3JN. Tel. 091-284 8448.

19. *Scotland East:* Belford House, 59 Belford Road, Edinburgh EH4 3UE. Tel. 031-225 1313.

20. *Scotland West:* 314 Vincent Street, Glasgow G3 8XG. Tel. 041-204 2646.

Children with special needs

Publications and organizations relating to specific activities are listed in the appropriate sections.

Appendix

Books and leaflets

Adam, R.C. *et al.* (1982) *Games, Sports and Exercises for the Physically Handicapped* (3rd edition), Philadelphia: Lea & Febiger.

British Epilepsy Association (n.d.) *Epilepsy: A Guide for Teachers*, Leeds: British Epilepsy Association.

Croucher, N. (1981) *Outdoor Pursuits for Disabled People* (2nd edition), London: Disabled Living Foundation.

Groves, L. (ed.) (1979) *Physical Education for Special Needs*, Cambridge: Cambridge University Press.

RoSPA, Safety Education Department, *Wheelchair Proficiency Award Scheme*, Birmingham: RoSPA.

Thomson, N. (ed.) (1984) *Sports and Recreation Provision for Disabled People*, London: Architectural Press, for Disabled Living Foundation.

Useful addresses

Asthma Research Council (also The Asthma Society and Friends of Asthma Research), 300 Upper Street, London N1 2XX. Tel. 01-226 2260.

British Diabetic Association, 10 Queen Anne Street, London W1M 0BD. Tel. 01-323 1531.

British Epilepsy Association, Anstey House, 40 Hanover Square, Leeds LS3 1BE. Tel. 0532 439393.

British Sports Association for the Disabled, Hayward House, Barnard Crescent, Aylesbury, Buckinghamshire HP21 8PP. Tel. 0296 27889.

Cystic Fibrosis Research Trust, 5 Blyth Road, Bromley, Kent BR1 3RS. Tel. 01-464 7211.

Haemophilia Society, 16 Trinity Street, London SE1 1DE. Tel. 01-407 1010.

Handicapped Adventure Playground Association, Fulham Palace, Bishops Avenue, London SW6 6EA. Tel. 01-736 4443.

The Multiple Sclerosis Society of Great Britain and Northern Ireland, 25 Effie Road, London SW6 1EE. Tel. 01-736 6267.

Muscular Dystrophy Group of Great Britain, Nattrass House, 35 Macaulay Road, Clapham, London SW4 0QP. Tel. 01-720 8055.

National Deaf Children's Society, 45 Hereford Road, London W2 5AH. Tel. 01-229 9272.

National Eczema Society, Tavistock House North, Tavistock Square, London WC1H 9SR. Tel. 01-388 4097.

The Partially Sighted Society, 206 Great Portland Street, London W1N 6AA. Tel. 01-387 8840.

Royal Association for Disablement and Rehabilitation (RADAR), 25 Mortimer Street, London W1N 8AB. Tel. 01-637 5400.

Royal National Institute for the Blind, 224 Great Portland Street, London W1N 6AA. Tel. 01-388 1266.

The Royal Society for the Prevention of Accidents (RoSPA), Cannon House, The Priory Queensway, Birmingham B4 6BS. Tel. 021-200 2461.

The Spastics Society, 12 Park Crescent, London W1N 4EQ. Tel. 01-636 5020.

Camping

Books and leaflets

Cade, R. (ed.) *Cade's Camping Site Guide* (published annually), Bletchley: Marwain Publishing.

Dominy, E. (1972) *Camping*, Teach Yourself Books, Sevenoaks: Hodder & Stoughton.

Fowler, E. (1987) *Camping* (3rd edition), Know the Game Series, produced in collaboration with The Camping and Caravanning Club, London: A. & C. Black.

Girl Guides Association (1987) *Health and Hygiene for Camps and Holidays*, London: Girl Guides Association.

Greenbank, A. (1979) *Camping for Young People*, London: Pan Books.

Robinson, D. (1981) *Backpacking*, E.P. Sport. London: A. & C. Black.

Rogers, A. (ed.) *Alan Rogers' Good Camps Guide for France* (published annually), Rottingdean: Deneway Guides & Travel. *Alan Rogers' Selected Sites for Caravanning and Camping in Europe* (published annually), Rottingdean: Deneway Guides & Travel. *Good Camps Guide: Guide to Recommended British Camp Sites for the Touring Caravanner and Camper* (published annually), Rottingdean: Deneway Guides & Travel.

Williams, B. (1978) *Camping*, London: Pan Books.

Williams, P.F. (1972) *Camping Complete*, London: Pelham Books.

Useful address

*The Camping and Caravanning Club Ltd, 11 Lower Grosvenor Place, London SW1W 0EY. Tel. 01-828 1012.

Caving

Books and leaflets

Cons, D. (1966) *Cavecraft*, London: Harrap.
Cullingford, C.H.D. (ed.) (1962) *British Caving*, London:
   Routledge & Kegan Paul.
   (1969) *Manual of Caving Techniques*. London: Routledge &
   Kegan Paul.
Jasinski, M. and Maxwell, B. (1968) *Caves and Caving*, London:
   Hamlyn.
Judson, D. and Champion, A. (1981) *Caving and Potholing*,
   London: Granada Publishing.
Lyon, B. (1983) *Venturing Underground*, London: A. & C. Black.
National Caving Association (n.d.) *National Caving Code* Swansea.

Useful addresses

*British Association of Caving Instructors. Secretary: 112
   Boundary Road, Carlisle, Cumbria CA2 4HT. Tel. 0228 47359.
*National Caving Association, The White Lion, Ynys Uchaf,
   Ystradgynlais, Swansea SA9 1RW. Tel. 0639 849 519.

Cycling

Books and leaflets

Ballantine, R. (1975) *Richard's Bicycle Book*, London: Pan Books.
Hughes, T. (1978) *Adventure Cycling in Britain*, Poole: Blandford
   Press.
Knottley, P. (1981) *Cycle Touring in Britain and the Rest of Europe*
   (2nd edition), London: Constable.
MacKenzie, J. (1981) *Cycling*, Oxford: Oxford University Press.
The Royal Society for the Prevention of Accidents (1986) *Bicycle
   Owner's Handbook* (revised edition), Birmingham: RoSPA.
Watson, R. and Gray, M. (1978) *Penguin Book of the Bicycle*,
   Harmondsworth: Penguin Books.

Useful addresses

British Cycling Federation, 16 Upper Woburn Place, London
   WC1H 0QE. Tel. 01-387 9320.

English Schools Cycling Association. General Secretary: P.A.W.
Dixon, 6 Malmers Well Road, High Wycombe,
Buckinghamshire HP13 6PD. Tel. 0494 446857.
The Royal Society for the Prevention of Accidents, National
Cycling Officer, Cannon House, The Priory Queensway,
Birmingham B4 6BS. Tel. 021-200 2461.

Field studies and countryside

Books and leaflets

Nature Conservancy Council (1982) *Wildlife, the Law and You*,
Peterborough: Nature Conservancy Council.

Useful addresses

Countryside Commission, John Dower House, Crescent Place,
Cheltenham, Gloucestershire GL50 3RA. Tel. 0242 521381.
Council for Environmental Education, School of Education,
University of Reading, London Road, Reading RG1 5AQ. Tel.
0734 875234.
National Association of Field Studies Officers. Secretary: P.
Greenough, Arnfield Tower Field Study Centre, Manchester
Road, Tintwistle, Hyde, Cheshire SK14 7NE. Tel. 04574 2420.
National Trust, 36 Queen Anne's Gate, London SW1H 9AS. Tel.
01-222 9251.
Nature Conservancy Council, Northminster House,
Peterborough PE1 1UA. Tel. 0733 40345.

Environment codes

Care of Our Coast, International Union for the Conservation of
Nature (c/o Council for Environmental Education, School of
Education, University of Reading, London Road, Reading
RG1 5AQ).
Code for Geological Field Work, Geologists' Association (Dr E.
Robinson, Librarian, Geologists' Association, c/o Geology
Department, University College, Gower Street, London
WC1E 6BT).
A Code for Insect Collecting, Joint Committee for the Conservation
of British Insects (Royal Entomological Society of London, 41
Queen's Gate, London SW7 5HU).
Code of Conduct for Conservation of Mosses and Liverworts, British
Bryological Society (Dr P.D. Coker, School of Biological

Sciences, Thames Polytechnic, Wellington Street, London
SE18 6PF).
Code of Conduct for the Conservation of Wild Plants, Botanical Society
of British Isles (c/o Department of Botany, British Museum
(Natural History), Cromwell Road, London, SW7 5BD).
Country Code, Countryside Commission (John Dower House,
Crescent Place, Cheltenham, Gloucestershire GL50 3RA).
Fieldwork Code, National Association of Field Studies Officers
(Secretary: P. Greenough, Arnfield Tower Field Study Centre,
Manchester Road, Tintwistle, Hyde, Cheshire SK14 7NE).
Geographical Fieldwork in Practice, Geographical Association (343
Fulwood Road, Sheffield S10 3BP).
The Nature Photographers' Code of Practice, Association of Natural
History Photographic Societies (c/o RSPB, The Lodge, Sandy,
Bedfordshire SG19 2DL).
Outdoor Studies Code, Council for Environmental Education
(School of Education, University of Reading, London Road,
Reading RG1 5AQ).
Safety in Biological Fieldwork, Institute of Biology (20 Queensbury
Place, London SW7 2DZ).
Visiting National Nature Reserves, Nature Conservancy Council
(Northminster House, Peterborough PE1 1UA).

Maps, orienteering, and weather

Books and leaflets

Brown, T.H.C. and Hunter, R.H. (1979) *Weather Lore* (2nd
edition), London: Spurbooks Venture Guides.
Disley, J. (1978) *Orienteering*, London: Faber.
(1971) *Your Way with Map and Compass*, London: Blond
Educational.
Kjellstrom, B. (1976) *Be Expert with Map and Compass: The
Orienteering Handbook*, New York: Scribners.
McNeill, C., Ramsden, J., and Renfrew, T. (1987) *Teaching
Orienteering: A Handbook for Teachers, Instructors and Coaches*,
Colchester: Harveys, in conjunction with the British
Orienteering Federation.
Marchington, T. (ed.) (1982) *Reading Maps*, Colour Units:
Geography, London: Macdonald Educational.
(1986) *The Weather*, Colour Units: Geography, London:
Macdonald Educational.
Palmer, P. (1976) *Orienteering for the Young*, Matlock: British

Orienteering Federation.
Porteans, B. (1978) *Orienteering*, Yeovil: Oxford Illustrated Press.
Watson, J.D. (1976) *Map Reading*, Know the Game series, London:
A. & C. Black.

Useful address

*British Orienteering Federation, Riversdale, Dale Road North,
Darley Dale, Matlock, Derbyshire DE4 2HX. Tel. 0629 734042.

Mountaineering

Books and leaflets

Barry, J. and Jepson, T. (1987) *Safety on Mountains* (2nd edition),
Manchester: British Mountaineering Council.
Brown, T.H.C. and Hunter, R.H. (1979) *Survival and Rescue* (2nd
edition), London Spurbooks Venture Guides.
British Mountaineering Council (n.d.) *Mountain Code*,
Manchester: British Mountaineering Council.
(n.d.) *Mountain Hypothermia*, Manchester: British
Mountaineering Council.
Cliff, P. (1986) *Mountain Navigation* (3rd edition) (available from P.
Cliff, Ardenberg, Grant Road, Grantown-on-Spey,
Morayshire PH26 3LD).
Langmuir, E. (1984) *Mountaincraft and Leadership*, Manchester:
Mountainwalking Leader Training Board, and Scottish Sports
Council.

Useful addresses

*British Mountaineering Council, Crawford House, Precinct
Centre, Booth Street East, Manchester M13 9RZ. Tel. 061-273
5163.
*Mountainwalking Leader Training Board, Crawford House,
Precinct Centre, Booth Street East, Manchester M13 9RZ. Tel.
061-273 5839.
*Scottish Mountain Leader Training Board, 1 St Colme Street,
Edinburgh EH3 6AA. Tel. 031-225 8411.
*Mountain Leader Training Board (Northern Ireland), Sports
Council for Northern Ireland, House of Sport, Upper Malone
Road, Belfast BT9 5LA. Tel. 0232 661222.

Appendix

Museums

Books and leaflets

HM Inspectorate, Department of Education and Science (1987) *A Survey of the Use Some Schools in Six Local Education Authorities Make of Museum Services*, London: HMSO.

Useful address

Group for Education in Museums. Secretary: Peter Divall, Kent County Council Museum Service, West Malling Air Station, West Malling, Kent ME19 6QE. Tel. 0732 845845.
Individual museums will supply details of their education service.

Riding

Books and leaflets

Bicknell, J., Henn, H., and Webb, J. (n.d.) *Guide to Riding*, Diamond Centre for Handicapped Riders (Woodmansterne Road, Carshalton, Surrey SM5 4DT).
The British Horse Society (1986) *Riding and Roadcraft* (6th edition), Kenilworth: The British Horse Society.

Useful addresses

*The British Horse Society, The British Equestrian Centre, Stoneleigh, Kenilworth, Coventry, Warwickshire CV8 2LR. Tel. 0203 52241.
Riding for the Disabled Association, Avenue T, National Agricultural Centre, Kenilworth, Warwickshire CV8 2LY. Tel. 0203 56107.

Skiing

Books and leaflets

Sunday Times (1982) *We Learned to Ski*, London: Collins.
Williams, R. (1984) *Ski Course Organizer Scheme Handbook*, Halesowen: English Ski Council.

Useful addresses

*The British Ski Federation, 118 Eaton Square, London SW1W
9AF. Tel. 01-235 8227.
*English Ski Council, Area Library Building, The Precinct,
Halesowen, West Midlands B63 4AJ. Tel. 021 501 2314.
*Ski Club of Great Britain, 118 Eaton Square, London SW1W
9AF. Tel. 01-245 1033.

Walking

Books, leaflets, and wallcharts

Department of Transport (n.d.) *Safety on Sponsored Walks*,
London: HMSO.
Lumley, P. (1980) *Hill Walking* (2nd revision edition), London:
Spurbooks Venture Guides.
The Ramblers Association, in conjunction with the Trustee
Savings Bank, (n.d.) *Discovering the Countryside* (4 wallcharts
and booklet). London: The Ramblers Association.
The Ramblers Association, in conjunction with the Trustee
Savings Bank, (n.d.) *Public Footpaths: A Natural Teaching
Resource*. London: The Ramblers Association.
Westacott, H.D. (1978) *The Walker's Handbook*, Harmondsworth:
Penguin Books.
Williams, P.F. (1979) *Hill Walking*, London: Pelham Books.

Useful addresses

*London Distance Walkers Association. Secretary: E. Bishop,
Lodgefield Cottage, High Street, Slimwell, Wadhurst, East
Sussex TN5 7PA. Tel. 0580 87341.
*The Ramblers Association, 1–5 Wandsworth Road, London SW8
2XX. Tel. 01-582 6826.

Water sports and activities

Books, leaflets, and audio-visual material

British Epilepsy Association (1987) *Swimming and Epilepsy*, Leeds:
British Epilepsy Association.
British Sports Association for the Disabled (1983) *Water Sports for
the Disabled*, London: A. & C. Black.

Appendix

British Sub Aqua Club (1982) *Snorkeler's Manual* (revised edition),
London: British Sub Aqua Club.

(1987) *Sport Diving*, London: Stanley Paul.

British Waterways Board (1986) *Be Water Wise*, tape/slide
presentation, London: British Waterways Board.

Brockhaus, P. and Stanciu, U. (1980) *Sailboarding, Basic and
Advanced Techniques* (2nd revised edition), London: Adlard
Coles.

Darwin, A. (1976) *Canals and Rivers of Britain*, London: Dent.

Edwards, L. (1985) *Inland Waterways of Great Britain* (6th edition,
revised and enlarged), Huntingdon: Imray, Laurie Norie &
Wilson.

Elkington, H. (1978) *Swimming: A Handbook for Teachers*,
Cambridge: Cambridge University Press.

Good, G.C. (ed.) (1983) *Canoeing Handbook*, Weybridge: British
Canoe Union.

Hazzard, J. (1982) *Instructors' Training Handbook*, London: British
Sub Aqua Club.

HM Coastguard (n.d.) *Boardsailing Safety Guide*, London: HMSO.

(n.d.) *Coastguards: The Coordinators*, London: HMSO.

(n.d.) *Small Craft Safety Checklist*, London: HMSO.

(n.d.) *Yacht and Boat Safety Scheme*, London: HMSO.

Marine Conservation Society (n.d.) *Underwater Conservation Code*,
leaflet and slides, Ross-on-Wye: Marine Conservation Society.

Reid, M.J. (1976) *Handling the Disabled Child in Water* (2nd edition),
Aberdeen: APCP Publications.

The Royal Life Saving Society, in conjunction with the Leeds
Permanent Building Society (1984) Aquapack Teacher's Kit 1
and 2, London: The Royal Life Saving Society.

in conjunction with the Leeds Permanent Building Society
(1984) *The Blue Code for Water Safety*, London: The Royal Life
Saving Society.

in conjunction with the Leeds Permanent Building Society
(1984) *Lifeline*. Video of approximately 20 minutes. (*Lifeline*
outlines the Aquapack scheme, and is available on loan from
branches of the Leeds Permanent Building Society.)

(1979) *Life Saving and Water Safety*, Studley: The Royal Life
Saving Society.

The Royal Society for the Prevention of Accidents, Water and
Leisure Safety Department (1985) *Be Water Wise Code*,
Birmingham: RoSPA.

(1986) *Water Wise Awareness Pack*, Birmingham: RoSPA.

Royal Yachting Association (1983) *National Dinghy Sailing Scheme:*

Syllabus and Logbook, Woking: Royal Yachting Association.
Sports Council and Water Recreation Division of Central Council
of Physical Recreation (n.d.) *Water Sports Code*, London:
CCPR.

Useful addresses

*Amateur Swimming Association, Harold Fern House, Derby
Square, Loughborough LE11 0AL. Tel. 0509 230431.

*British Canoe Union, Flexel House, 45–57 High Street,
Addlestone, Weybridge, Surrey KT15 1JV. Tel. 0932 41341.

British Schools Canoeing Association (address as British Canoe
Union).

*British Sub Aqua Club, 16 Upper Woburn Place, London WC1H
0QW. Tel. 01-387 9302.

British Waterways Board, Melbury House, Melbury Terrace,
London NW1 6JY. Tel. 01-262 6711.

English Schools Swimming Association. Hon. General Secretary:
D. Redman, 3 Maybank Grove, Aigburth, Liverpool L17 6DW.
Tel. 051-427 3707.

HM Coastguard, Department of Transport, Room 8/1, Sunley
House, High Holborn, London WC1V 6LP. Tel. 01-405 6911.

*Inland Waterways Association, 114 Regents Park Road, London
NW1 8UQ. Tel. 01-586 2556.

Marine Conservation Society, 4 Gloucester Road, Ross-on-Wye,
Herefordshire HR9 5BU. Tel. 0989 66017.

National School Sailing Association. Hon. Secretary: D.G. Sykes,
Erw Fair, Marton cum Grafton, York YO9 5QY. Tel. 090 12
2818.

*The Royal Life Saving Society, Mountbatten House, Studley,
Warwickshire B80 7NN. Tel. 052 785 3943.

*Royal Yachting Association, Victoria Way, Woking, Surrey
GU21 1EQ. Tel. 048 62 5022.

The Water and Leisure Safety Department, The Royal Society for
the Prevention of Accidents, Cannon House, The Priory,
Queensway, Birmingham B4 6BS. Tel. 021-200 2461.

Work Experience

Books and leaflets

Department of Education and Science (n.d.) *Work Experience*,
Circular 7/74, London: HMSO.

Appendix

Jamieson, I., Newman, R., and Peffers, J. for the School Curriculum Industry Partnership (1986) *Work Experience Workbooks: a Critical Review*, York: Longman for SCDC Publications.

Watts, A.G. for the School Curriculum Industry Partnership (1986) *Work Shadowing*, York: Longman for SCDC Publications

Watts, A.G. for the School Curriculum Industry Partnership (1987) *Executive Shadows*, York: Longman for SCDC Publications.

Useful addresses

School Curriculum Industry Partnership, (SCIP) Newcombe House, 45 Notting Hill Gate, London W11 3JB. Tel. 01–229 1234.

Trident Trust, Robert Hyde House, 48 Bryanston Square, London W1A 1BQ. Tel. 01–723 3281.

Understanding British Industry, Centre Point, 103 New Oxford Street, London WC1A WDU. Tel. 01–379 7400 *and at* Sun Alliance House, New Inn Hall Street, Oxford OX1 2QE. Tel. 0865 722585.

National Parks

Useful addresses

Brecon Beacons National Park: Information Officer, 7 Glamorgan Street, Brecon, Powys LD3 7DP. Tel. 0874 4437.

Brecon Beacons National Park Information Centres: Monk Street, Abergavenny, Gwent NP7 5NA (3254 0873); Watton Mount, Brecon, Powys LD3 7DF (0874 4437); Broad Street, Llandovery, Dyfed SA20 0AR (0550 20693). Mountain Centre: Nr Libanus, Brecon, Powys LD3 8ER (0874 3366).

Dartmoor National Park: The National Park Officer, Parke, Haytor Road, Bovey Tracey, Devon TQ13 9JQ. Tel. 0626 832093.

Exmoor National Park, Exmoor House, Dulverton, Somerset TA22 9HL. Tel. 0398 23665.

Lake District National Park: Youth and Schools Liaison Officer, Brockhole, National Park Centre, Windermere, Cumbria LA23 1LJ. Tel. 096 62 6601.

The Moors Centre, Danby, Whitby, North Yorkshire YO21 2NB.
Tel. 0287 60540.

Northumberland National Park: Information Officer, Eastburn,
South Park, Hexham, Northumberland NE46 1BS. Tel. 0434
605555.

North York Moors National Park: Information Officer, The Old
Vicarage, Bondgate, Helmsley, Yorkshire YO6 5BP. Tel. 0439
70657.

Peak National Park Study Centre: Youth and Schools Liaison
Officer, Losehill Hall, Castleton, Derbyshire S30 2WB. Tel.
0433 20373.

Pembrokeshire Coast National Park: Assistant Information
Officer, County Planning Department, County Offices,
Haverfordwest, Dyfed SA61 1QZ. Tel. 0437 3131.

Snowdonia Park: Youth and Schools Liaison Officer, Yr Hen
Ysgol, Maentwrog, Blaenau Ffestiniog, Gwynedd LL48 6LS.
Tel. 076 685 274.

Yorkshire Dales National Park: National Park Officer,
Yorebridge House, Bainbridge, Leyburn, North Yorkshire
DL8 3BP. Tel. 0969 50456.

British Isles tourist boards

Useful addresses

Cumbria Tourist Board, Ashleigh, Holly Road, Windermere,
Cumbria LA23 2AQ. Tel. 096 62 4444.

East Anglia Tourist Board, Toppesfield Hall, Hadleigh, Suffolk
IP7 5DN. Tel. 0473 822922.

East Midlands Tourist Board, Exchequergate, Lincoln LN2 1PZ.
Tel. 0522 31521.

English Tourist Board, Thames Tower, Black's Road,
Hammersmith, London W6 9EL. Tel. 01-846 9000.

Heart of England Tourist Board, 2–4 Trinity Street, Worcester
WR1 2PW. Tel. 0905 29511.

Irish Tourist Board, Ireland House, 150 New Bond Street,
London W1Y 0AQ. Tel. 01-493 3201.

Isle of Man Tourist Board, 13 Victoria Street, Douglas, Isle of
Man. Tel. 0624 74323.

Isle of Wight Tourist Board, 21 High Street, Newport, Isle of
Wight PO30 1JS. Tel. 0983 524343.

London Tourist Board, 26 Grosvenor Gardens, London SW1W

0DU. Tel. 01-730 3488. Tourist Information Centre, Victoria Station Forecourt, London SW1.

Northern Ireland Tourist Board, River House, 48 High Street, Belfast BT1 2DS. Tel. 0232 231221. Also 11 Berkeley Street, London W1K 6BU. Tel. 01-493 0601.

Northumbria Tourist Board, 9 Osborne Terrace Jesmond, Newcastle upon Tyne NE2 1NT. Tel. 0632 817744.

North West Tourist Board, The Last Drop Village, Bromley Cross, Bolton, Lancs BL7 9PZ. Tel. 0204 591511.

Scottish Tourist Board, 23 Ravelston Terrace, Edinburgh EH4 3EU. Tel. 031-332 2433. Also 19 Cockspur Street, SW1Y 5BL. Tel. 01-930 8661.

South East England Tourist Board, 1 Warwick Park, Tunbridge Wells, Kent TN2 5TA. Tel. 0892 40766.

Southern Tourist Board, Town Hall Centre, Leigh Road, Eastleigh, Hants SO5 4DE. Tel. 0703 616027.

States of Jersey Tourism Committee, Weighbridge, St Helier, Jersey, C.I. Tel. 0534 24779. Also Jersey Tourist Information Office, 35 Albemarle Street, London W1X 3FB. Tel. 01-493 5278.

Thames and Chilterns Tourist Board, 8 The Market Place, Abingdon, Oxon OX14 3UD. Tel. 0235 22711.

Wales Tourist Board, Brunel House, 2 Fitzalan Road, Cardiff CF2 1UY. Tel. 0222 499909. Also Wales Centre, 34 Piccadilly, London W1V 9PB. Tel. 01-409 0969.

West Country Tourist Board, Trinity Court, 37 Southernhay East, Exeter, Devon EX1 1QS. Tel. 0392 76351.

Yorkshire and Humberside Tourist Board, 312 Tadcaster Road, York, North Yorkshire YO2 2HF. Tel. 0904 707961.

Other tourist boards

Useful addresses

Austrian National Tourist Office, 30 St George Street, London W1R 9FA. Tel. 01-629 0461.

Belgian National Tourist Office, 38 Dover Street, London W1X 3RB. Tel. 01-499 5379.

Danish Tourist Board, Sceptre House, 169–73 Regent Street, London W1R 8PY. Tel. 01-734 2637.

French Government Tourist Office, 178 Piccadilly, London W1V 0AL. Tel. 01-499 6911.

German National Tourist Office, 61 Conduit Street, London
W1R 0EW. Tel. 01-734 2600.
Greek Tourist Agency, 320 Regent Street, London W1R 8DL. Tel.
01-580 3152.
(Hungary) Danube Travel Agency, 6 Conduit Street, London
W1R 9TG. Tel. 01-493 0263.
Icelandair, 73 Grosvenor Street, London W1X 9DP. Tel. 01-499
9971.
Italian State Tourist Office, 1 Princes Street, London W1R 8AY.
Tel. 01-408 1254.
Netherlands Board of Tourism, Egginton House, 25–28
Buckingham Gate, London SW1E 6LD. Tel. 01-630 0451.
Norwegian Tourist Board, 20 Pall Mall, London SW1Y 5NE. Tel.
01-839 6255.
Spanish National Tourist Office, 57–58 St James's Street, London
SW1A 1LD. Tel. 01-499 0901.
Swedish National Tourist Office, 3 Cork Street, London W1X
1HA. Tel. 01-437 5816.
Swiss Tourist Office, Swiss Centre, 1 New Coventry Street,
London W1V 3HG. Tel. 01-734 1921.
Yugoslav National Tourist Office, 143 Regent Street, London
W1R 8AE. Tel. 01-734 5243.

Travel abroad

Books and leaflets

The Central Bureau (1987) *Home from Home*, London: The
Central Bureau.
(published annually) *Working Holiday*, London: The Central
Bureau.
Customs and Excise Department (May 1986) *How to go through
British Customs*, Customs Notice No. 1 (from CDE5 Branch),
London: HMSO.
Department of Health and Social Security, *Medical Costs Abroad:
what you need to know before you go*, Leaflet SA30, DHSS (from
local DHSS Office or, if bulk order, from DHSS Leaflets, P.O.
Box 21, Stanmore, Middlesex HA7 1AY. Tel. 01-952 2311).
National Association of Head Teachers Council (April 1973)
Memorandum on School Journeys Abroad, London: NAHT.
(1984) *Memorandum on Supervision*, London: NAHT.
Quilter, R. (ed.) (1985) *The Touring Guide to Europe*, Ashbourne:
Moorland Publishing.

Spearing, P. (1986) *Your School Journey Abroad*, London: New
 Education Press.
Standing Conference of Youth Organizations (1984) *Home and
 Away*, Standing Conference of Youth Organizations, Belfast
 (86 Lisburn Road, Belfast BT9 6AF).
Youth Exchange Centre (1986) *Help?! Guidelines on International
 Youth Exchange* (7th edition), London: Youth Exchange
 Centre.

Useful addresses

The Central Bureau, Seymour Mews House, Seymour Mews,
 London W1H 9PC. Tel. 01-486 5101.
YHA Services, 14 Southampton Street, London WC2E 7HY. Tel.
 01-836 7615.

Passport offices

London: Clive House, 70–8 Petty France, London SW1H 9HD.
 Tel. 01-279 3434.
Liverpool: 5th Floor, India Buildings, Water Street, Liverpool L2
 0QZ. Tel. 051-237 3010.
Newport: Olympia House, Upper Dock Street, Newport, Gwent.
 Tel. 0633 244292.
Peterborough: 55 Westfield Road, Westwood, Peterborough PE3
 6TG. Tel. 0733 895555.
Belfast: Hampton House, 47 High Street, Belfast BT1 2QS. Tel.
 0232 232371.

Government departments

Customs & Excise Department, Dorset House, Stamford Street,
 London SE1 9PS. Tel. 01-928 0533.
Department of Education and Science, Elizabeth House, York
 Road, London SE1 7PH. Tel. 01-934 9000.
Department of Education, Northern Ireland, Rathgael House,
 Balloo Road, Bangor, Co Down, BT19 2PR.

Advisory Group Members

Pat Belshaw, HMI: Department of Education and Science

John Blackmore: Somerset LEA

David Brierley: Professional Association of Teachers

Frank Carter: Education Consultant

Collette Crossen: Priesthorpe School, Leeds

Peter Gedling: Dorset LEA
Society of Education Officers

Ken Gill: Central Council of Physical Recreation

Anne Hillyard: Castleford High School, Wakefield

Wally Keay: Safety and Technical Committee, Duke of Edinburgh's Award Scheme

Gordon Macgregor: British Association of Advisers and Lecturers in Physical Education

John Miller: Walsall LEA
National Association for Outdoor Education
National Panel of Advisers in Outdoor Education

Eric Mullineux: National Confederation of Parent-Teacher Associations

Eric Pilkington: National Association of Headteachers

Jean Roberts: Health Education Authority, Initial Teacher Education Project

John Rowe: National Union of Teachers

John Rowland:	National Association of Schoolmasters/Union of Women Teachers
Keith Smith:	Secondary Heads Association
Mark Stedman:	Assistant Masters and Mistresses Association
Jane Valentine:	National Council for Voluntary Youth Services
Deborah Williams:	Royal Society for the Prevention of Accidents

INDEX

www.ingramcontent.com/pod-product-compliance
Ingram Content Group UK Ltd.
Pitfield, Milton Keynes, MK11 3LW, UK
UKHW041839280225
455677UK00010B/252